Praise for Cohen's previous works:

Praise from the experts:

BREAK THE RULES

The Secret Code to Finding a Great Job Fast

WILLIAM A. COHEN, Ph.D.

Prentice Hall Press

Library of Congress Cataloging-in-Publication Data

Cohen, William A.
　　Break the rules : the secret to finding a great job fast / William A. Cohen.
　　　　p. cm.
　　Includes index.
　　ISBN 0-7352-0201-X (pbk.)
　　　1. Job hunting.　I. Title.
　　HF5382.7.C628 2001
　　650.14—dc21

00-068469

Acquisitions Editor: *Tom Power*
Production Editor: *Jacqueline Roulette*
Formatting/Interior Design: *Publications Development Company*

© 2001 by William A. Cohen

Printed in the United States of America

10　9　8　7　6　5　4　3　2　1

ISBN 0-7352-0201-X

 **Prentice Hall Press** Paramus, NJ 07652

http://www.phdirect.com

Contents

About the Author

D r. Cohen is professor of marketing, the chair of the marketing department at California State University Los Angeles and the author of 37 professional business and textbooks translated into eleven languages. Two of these (1985 and 1989) were selected by *The Library Journal* as a "Best Business Book of the Year." In 1998, *Management General,* the cyber magazine, nominated one of Dr. Cohen's books as one of the ten best management books of the year.

Dr. Cohen has been a practicing headhunter as well as a corporate executive. He has used his own techniques in industry, and used them to get his position as a professor as well. His extensive research into job finding has resulted in "cutting-edge" concepts. His integration and use of techniques from business, marketing, sales, and psychology have resulted in a powerful system which has helped thousands of new graduates, professionals, and senior executives "get a great job fast."

Dr. Cohen has a BS in engineering from the United States Military Academy, an MBA from the University of Chicago, and an MA and PhD in management from the Peter Drucker School of Management, Claremont Graduate University. Dr. Cohen is also a distinguished graduate of the Industrial College of the Armed Forces, National Defense University, Washington, D.C. and is a retired Major General from the USAF Reserve.

Introduction

"Dr. Cohen's system is replete with effective tips that may surprise even the most experienced of job hunters."

—The Chicago Tribune

Peter Drucker is perhaps the greatest management thinker of our age. I had the good fortune to have Drucker as the major professor in my doctoral program from 1975 to 1979 at Claremont Graduate School, now the Peter F. Drucker School of Management at Claremont Graduate University. I have called on Drucker for advice and help ever since. Although the lessons I learned from Peter are, and continue to be, numerous, none is more pervasive than his deep belief that what "everyone knows" is usually wrong.

My work with job seekers, from recent college undergraduates to out-of-work CEOs, presidents, and former high ranking military officers, has led me to conclude that this is especially true in job finding. "Everyone knows" that you must send a nicely printed resume out in order to get a job. Yet, my work with others and my own experience demonstrate conclusively that the time-honored resume, no matter how well done, usually will hurt the job seeker's chances of "getting a great job fast." Similarly, following the instructions demanded in job advertisements, applying for a job through the human resource department, letting prospective employers control the job interview, providing references on request, and even posting one's resume on the internet, are almost always the wrong thing to do from the job seeker's perspective. They will all hurt your chances of getting the job that you want at the compensation that you want, even though "everyone knows" this is what you must do.

Why are the rules of job finding so terribly wrong? I believe this is due to several reasons. First, although our ability to find a good job has a significant impact on success or failure in our careers, few schools give academic credit, require the standards demanded in our professional training for education about job seeking, or encourage professors to do research about job finding. So, a university might require much from its students in the way of math, English, or nuclear engineering, but the best it will do for an education in job finding is a few workshops through a career development center. The workshops are optional and hardly academically rigorous. Thus, unlike other subjects taught at the university, the discipline of job finding is neither well researched nor rigorous. We graduate, somehow get a job and forget about it. Some years later, we find ourselves in need of job-finding help. We stick with the same old rules we remember.

In our grandparents' day, looking for new work in mid-career was rare. Until the great depression, folks generally worked in one company for life. Even twenty years ago, the statistics were that you only worked in an average of four companies over a lifetime career. That's not true anymore. Technology has changed everything. The vinyl record industry provides a dramatic example. To put it succinctly, a $500 billion dollar industry completely disappeared within a year. Thousands of workers, managers, and professionals needed to find new jobs. They relied on what "everyone knew." Some got jobs after a time. Some never did. We aren't just company-hopping today. Technology has forced many of us to career-hop.

Another reason the rules are wrong is that they are given from the perspective of someone other than the job seeker. For example, from a human resource manager's perspective, a chronological resume is ideal. Why? Then, he or she can more easily screen out applicants he *thinks* fail to meet the qualifications desired by the decision-maker (your future boss). One problem is in the assumption that the human resource manager knows exactly what the decision-maker wants. This is rarely true, even when the human resource manager is intelligent and committed. Most are overworked and are handling multiple job searches. Frequently, the decision-maker doesn't want to spend a lot of time explaining his real needs, or the kind of individual he works best with. Much of what your prospective employer really needs in a subordinate cannot be documented. It's not easy to document a personality and the chemistry that must exist between boss and subordinate in a job situation.

Moreover, unless you send a book containing your life history, which the human resource manager wouldn't have time to read anyway, how can anyone determine completely whether or not you meet any requirement that a human resource manager has received second-hand from the decision-maker?

I wrote this book to teach you how to break the rules and to help you through a process that few of us train for, yet all of us must go through and on which a good deal of our success depends.

The first time I looked for a job, I didn't even know where to begin. I had been out of school for eleven years, and I had spent those years not in industry, but in the Air Force. Moreover, since I graduated from West Point, Uncle Sam had a guaranteed job for me on my graduation. Many friends who were not searching for new jobs told me it would be easy. But observation told me otherwise. I saw many extremely well-qualified people forced to take much lower positions than I knew they deserved. Yet, a few individuals always seemed to do well and consistently found good jobs. It took me several years to discover that, regardless of a person's qualifications, certain techniques are essential for successful job hunting. Amazingly, many were counter-intuitive and most went against the established rules.

Since my first experience in job hunting, I have examined countless books on the subject. Several were worth reading; others gave advice that could lead only to disaster. All had one major shortcoming: although the authors claimed years of experience related to job placement, none had relevant job-finding experience of their own.

I believe my qualifications for writing this book are unique. After my initial job seeking experience, I became a practicing manager in industry. I held positions as an engineering and marketing manager in companies large and small, foreign and domestic. I hired many, from secretary through senior manager. Then I became an executive recruiter or "headhunter." For the last twenty-one years I have been a university professor and I have conducted research into job finding techniques, as well as assisted the campaigns of my graduate and undergraduate students and many professionals and executives. Much of my research has been devoted to the application of marketing and sales techniques to job finding. In sum, I know the secrets of the professional headhunter as well as those of potential employers, but I have no vested interest and no reason not to reveal to you every secret that I know. Beyond that, I have the research and experience of hundreds of campaigns in which I participated.

Let me give you an example. No other book that I know of tells you the technique that professionals use to break a "blind" advertisement. The reason is simple. If everybody uses it, it won't work. Yet this technique can be crucial to the job hunter who must conduct a campaign in secret.

The fact that I am a university professor and not an employment counselor, human resource manager, executive recruiter, or college placement director also means that I see things from your viewpoint, not someone else's. I once read a book on job hunting written by a human resource manager. It recommended techniques that would have hurt your chances of finding a job. Why should this be so? Human resource managers play a unique role in hiring. Except in their own specialty, they cannot hire you, only prevent you from being hired. One of their main functions in hiring is to screen out candidates they feel are unsuited for a particular job. As I explained earlier, most personnel managers assume that they know best whether your background will allow you to perform a job adequately. So it is not surprising that a job-hunting book written by such a manager would recommend that you give information on your background that is not in your best interest to give. To be quite blunt, in many job-hunting situations it is to your advantage to sidestep personnel managers, human resource managers, whatever title they go by, or to manipulate them to your own advantage.

In another book, the president of an employment agency recommended that you state your minimum salary right in your resume. What's wrong with this? If your minimum is too high, you will probably be eliminated without an interview. Yet if you could get to the interview you might persuade an employer to pay more for your valuable services. If your stated minimum is well below the range for the job, you may also be eliminated. Many employers assume that you are not "heavy" enough for the job if the salary you want is too modest. Further, even if you get an interview and a job offer, your ability to negotiate is limited.

Why would an employment agency recommend doing this? Employment agencies get paid by the hiring companies only if they hire. Therefore they generally prefer to work with candidates who are relatively easy to place. One consideration, of course, is the willingness to accept a salary that is not too high for a particular job or industry. Further, an employment agency that is working a "fee paid" job order is working primarily for the company, not for you. So it is in the agency's interest to know the minimum amount you will accept. If this figure is known, the company certainly isn't going to offer you a lot more.

Many people from all walks of life used my previous books on job finding. *Business Week* called *The Executive's Guide to Finding a Superior Job* (now out of print) "the headhunter's favorite." Other endorsers, including *The Chicago Tribune,* while applauding one book, noted that my approach was "no-holds-barred." This is true. I felt this was only fair. For too long employers have maintained a totally unfair relationship with potential employees. Employers felt justified in lying, or in telling employees only half-truths. On the other hand, they expected job applicants to be both completely truthful, and dedicated to whatever slim hope they might hold out for a potential position. They delighted in keeping job applicants on a string and even in tricking them if they thought there was some advantage to be gained by doing so.

One corporate recruiter who visited my university every year for seven years was quite candid. In seven years, he never hired a single applicant. "You have to understand," he told me. "I visit hundreds of schools every year. I probably see thousands of students. Yet I only have a handful of jobs available."

A headhunter once told me how he hired a perfectly happy executive away from one company for a six-month job with another. The job was crucial, but would last only six months because the company was being sold. "Why would anybody leave a company where he was happy for a six-month job?," I asked. "We paid him pretty well," he answered, "and the company never told him that it was going to be being sold."

Not all companies and headhunters are so unethical, but some are. And until you are actually hired, most corporations view you as one of "them." They consider it an adversarial relationship, whether they are willing to admit it or not. With their power and a seemingly unending supply of job seekers, the odds are stacked against you—and corporations like it that way. My techniques not only allow you to defend yourself, they give you tremendous advantages over other job hunters.

Still, I don't want you to sacrifice your ethics, and you will not have to do so. But the weapons I give you are not insignificant. What I wrote in other books enraged some professional organizations. The American Psychology Association was very unhappy when I explained how to beat the tests that potential new hires are sometimes required to take. Associations of personnel managers weren't happy that I told job hunters how to go around them and right to the hiring executive. Let me tell you, when I've encountered some of these folks individually they are in 100% agreement with my methods . . . and they use them themselves when they look for jobs!

The techniques I will teach you in this book will help you to get a great job whether you are currently employed or have just resigned; whether you've been fired, laid off, or are a new graduate; whether you are young or old, handicapped, male or female, white, black, brown, red, yellow, or blue; or whether you are currently in industry, academia, government, or the military. I will introduce you to managers, recent graduates, and top executives who have made these techniques pay off. I will show you exactly how they did it. I am not instructing you in these techniques second-hand or through someone else's placement. When I was a practicing manager, several times I chose to resign my former job before searching for a new one. Yet I never took a new job without a substantial salary increase. As a matter of fact, I increased my own salary by 67 percent over one four-year period by using only a few of the techniques I will teach you in this book. And yes, I used the same techniques to get my position as a university professor.

So get ready. I am going to show you professional, no-holds-barred job-hunting techniques, some of which are little known outside the personnel placement industry, and others that are cutting-edge research that have never been applied to a job search except by a select few. Many of these techniques are being published for the first time. I will instruct you on how to plan your job-hunting campaign over a realistic period of time. I will tell you, for each phase of your campaign and for each technique, exactly what results you can expect. I will explain psychological testing and tell you how to do well when testing is a requirement. I will show you how to establish your overall career objective and how to pick your next job for maximum impact on your career. I will assist you in developing a superior resume and guide you in using it effectively, *without sending your resume to everyone* (in fact, sending out your resume will usually work against you—it's one of the rules you will break). I will teach you every method of getting job interviews, instruct you in how to train for them, and make you an expert interviewee. I will detail the secrets of how to make use of headhunters, personnel managers, hiring executives, and other "players" you will meet during your campaign. I will show you how to maintain control of the hiring situation until you get the great job that you want. I will show you how to use the internet without posting a resume anywhere. In sum, I will describe every important rule of job hunting that you must break in order to succeed.

A job campaign is like business itself. Your potential employer is the customer. You are the product. Other executives who are seeking the same job are your competition. In this book you will learn how to satisfy your customer and beat the competition. You will learn how to consistently find great jobs . . . fast.

You are about to start on an exciting adventure. This is an adventure that can easily be as exciting and as enlightening as any undertaken by "Indiana Jones." Moreover, you will complete it as a more confident person and with more control over your work life than you have ever had before. Happy hunting!

William A. Cohen, PhD
Pasadena

BREAK THE RULE

**BEGIN YOUR CAMPAIGN
WHEN YOU NEED A JOB**

1

HOW TO START YOUR CAMPAIGN FOR YOUR NEXT JOB ON THE FIRST DAY OF YOUR PRESENT JOB

"The sales campaign strategy as taught in your book is excellent because it focuses your energies and causes you to target companies and go after what you want. After getting laid off after many years with one firm, I didn't know where to begin. I really loved how you encourage your students to think big and have faith in our abilities and do all the practical and creative foundational things necessary to support such dreams. Thanks to you, I got an even better job in a few weeks."

—Marketing Manager with an International Accounting Firm

Conventional wisdom is that you begin your job campaign when you need a job. There is an inherent logic about this statement that seems irrefutable. The truth is that if you wait until you need a job to begin your job campaign, you are putting yourself at a significant disadvantage. Why? To run the most job effective campaign in the shortest possible time, you will need:

- Expert knowledge of your industry and its movers and shakers
- A reputation of high performance within the company
- A reputation of expertise in your field outside the company
- Colleagues, and even bosses who are willing to recommend you
- Reliable contacts outside the company to help you as references and with job intelligence

To acquire all this takes time. Therefore, begin to prepare for your next job campaign on the day you go to work in your new job.

All preparation falls into two categories: internal and external.

● INTERNAL PREPARATION

Internal preparation is that done within the company which will begin to prepare you for your next job. The very first thing you want to do is to learn everything you can about your present job, and to perform it to the very best of your ability. Once you learn your job, look for opportunities to learn other jobs in your company as well. You can do this by volunteering to help others with their jobs when needed. You can also volunteer to work on your own time, after work, and without additional pay to learn an additional job or to help out. If an opportunity comes up to actually do work in this other area, take it.

Certain other unpaid jobs will also become available from time to time. These will occur at all levels in the organization, from annual savings bond managers to membership on committees looking at compensation or stock options. Volunteers are always needed. Especially seek jobs that lead to contacts outside of your immediate group, and in particular those that put you in positions of leadership.

If all this activity happens to get you promoted in addition to preparing you to get a great job fast, so be it.

● EXTERNAL PREPARATION

Internal preparation works fine as far as getting you the preparation you need for your next job, but it doesn't go far enough. If you really want to get a great job fast, than you need to prepare yourself externally, as well. You must become known in your profession and in your industry outside of your company. How can you do this? It's easy.

Every profession and industry has associations that you can join. To prepare yourself to get a great job fast, you should not only join them, you should become active in them. Go to both local and national meetings. If your company won't pay your way, use your vacation time and go to the annual meeting on your own ticket. But don't just go . . . again, become active. Volunteer both locally and nationally and serve in leadership positions. If there is a newsletter or a journal, write for it. If there are other magazines read by those in your profession and industry, write for them, too.

You should also contribute to and meet with the leaders of your community whenever you can. This contribution can take many forms, from volunteer service in your church, synagogue, or mosque, to other ways of helping out in your community.

Now I know what you are thinking. All this and I'm supposed to have a life, too? The answer is yes. And if you doubt me, look around you at the really successful people. You will see that they are involved with all these things. This will take some time management, but you will find many of these activities to be synergistic. For example, that you are an officer in one organization will help you in running another or in doing your job. But pick and choose. No, you may not be able to do everything, but you can do a lot more than you imagined once you have decided to take your preparation for your next job seriously.

Again, your company may like it and promote you. I can't help that. I'm just trying to get you ready to get a great job fast when you need to.

● AN ACCOMPLISHMENT LOG

Every time you do something as a part of your job, or in a temporary job you have volunteered for, or anything else, write it down. Try to quantify these as accomplishments with little notes whenever you can. "Head of fund-raising committee for the church. Raised $10,000." You'll need all this later.

● WHAT IF IT IS TOO LATE . . . YOU NEED A JOB TODAY?

What if your situation is that you got fired, laid off, or quit your job today. Is all lost? No, it is not. But you need to get hold of yourself and organize a campaign plan right from the start.

● YOUR CAMPAIGN PLAN IS YOUR ROAD MAP TO SUCCESS

Once you have decided on the kind of job you want, you face the problem of getting from where you are now to the point where you accept the offer of a great job. If you were traveling to a place you had never been to before, you would get there most easily and most expeditiously by using a road map. In going from your present job (or unemployment) to the position of your choice, you will also use a road map. This road map is the *campaign plan.*

The campaign plan for job hunting will guide you to logical and effective courses of action, just as other types of plans guide you in reaching objectives on the job. The campaign plan for job hunting has been designed to enable you to get the job you want in the shortest possible time. Do not embark on a job campaign without first developing a plan as outlined in this chapter. If you do, you will remain on your job hunt longer and will limit the range of jobs available to you.

Any job campaign consists of three phases:

1. The preinterview phase
2. The interview phase
3. The postinterview phase

Note that the description of these phases clearly emphasizes the interview. This is done to focus on your real objective. Your first major objective is to get the interview. You won't get an offer until you do. Once you've been given the opportunity to interview, your next objective is to handle the interview successfully. Successful interviewing means that you sell your prospective employer (PE) on hiring your services. This puts you in a position to get the job offer. Your final objective is to negotiate that offer successfully.

Every campaign is different, reflecting different job objectives as well as different professional career goals. You must tailor your campaign to your particular situation. Your campaign plan is both a plan and an overview of the entire procedure.

● THE PREINTERVIEW PHASE OF YOUR CAMPAIGN

Preparing *Your* Resume

In Chapter 5 I'm going to tell you not to send your resume to anyone. At least not until after the interview. But you will need an ongoing, living, frequently updated resume so you will really understand you and what you have to offer. The basis of this resume will take you two to three days to get all your materials together and write. Once you do, you will have all the data you need to:

- Write sales letters with at least five major accomplishments in support of your job objective which you can send out in letter form, by fax, or by e-mail. I show you how to do this in Chapter 7 and give you examples in Appendix B.
- Prepare responses to advertisements that are right on target but disregard certain requirements in the ad. I'll tell you about those in Chapter 8.
- Prepare special resumes of your experiences that slant your accomplishments to the requirements of the job.

Writing Sales Letters

It will take you two to four days to develop sales letters that support your job objectives and to mail them to both PEs and executive recruiters.

Printing Letterheads for Your Sales Letters and Envelopes

Printing your letterheads and envelopes depends on your printer. This can take up to two weeks. If you shop around a little, you should be able to find a printer who can do the job in a week or less. If you have a laser printer and suitable fonts this can take much less time and money. However, if you want to go first class, you will have your letterheads done with a process called *thermographing*. That way it looks like engraving, but you'll need to go to a printer for this.

Obtaining Mailing Lists, Fax or E-mail Lists

You should start with a list of 1,000 companies, any one of which you would be prepared to work for if aspects of the job met your requirements. I'll tell you how to develop your list in Appendix C. You do not need to know everything about these companies. Just make sure they fit your basic requirements based on what you know about them. For example, if you are looking only for a large company, you shouldn't have any small companies on your list. You will also need a similar list of executive recruiters. Preparing these lists can take several days of somewhat tedious work.

Mailing Your Letters

Mailing sales letters includes the following mundane, but necessary chores: typing the PE's name and address on both sales letters and envelopes, signing the letters, sealing and stamping the envelopes, and mailing. If you do these tasks yourself, you could spend about 5 hours per 100 letters. Therefore, if you mail sales letters to 1,000 companies and 500 executive recruiters, you can estimate 75 hours of work, or roughly nine days to complete this part of the job. Similarly, if you are going to fax or send out your sales letters electronically, there is some routine work which cannot be avoided. Consider getting some family assistance if possible, or even hiring some part-time help. Still, when you remember that the job you will obtain will be a great job, much better than you would get normally, the effort and added expense is well worth it.

Answering Advertisements

Begin to collect job advertisements the day you decide to look for a job, but don't start responding until you get your sales letters out. More than likely, you will not start answering ads until the beginning of the third week. Don't worry about this "lost time." As explained fully in Chapter 8, the fact that you answer ads "late" is usually not a disadvantage.

Practicing Using the Telephone

After you have caught up on your ad answering and have it under control, start a telephone training program. You should maintain the program for as long as it takes you to become comfortable and proficient in speaking with PE-related people on the telephone. I show you how in Chapter 9.

Shoot for talking with twenty executives (not their secretaries) per day. Try to get at least one interview a day this way. If you follow this regime every weekday for two weeks, you will have talked with 200 executives; and if you have done it right, you will have lined up at least ten interviews. These are not the kind of interviews you may have had in the past. These are quality interviews, with a good chance that you'll get a job offer.

Meeting with Employment Agencies and Headhunters

Start setting up interviews with employment agencies and headhunters at the same time you begin your training with the telephone. Do not interview with more than five agencies unless it is for a specific job. Otherwise, your resume is likely to be scattered throughout your potential job market. Like most products that appear to be in great supply, you will not have the image of being in much demand.

Keeping Records of Sales Letter Results

Your record keeping will begin with the receipt of "rejects" about one to two weeks after you mail your first batch of sales letters. You will use these records to update your list of names (several executives will have resigned, retired, or been fired or transferred), and to start building a new mailing list of executives for a second mailing. Your records will show you how effective your sales letters are and whether you should revise them before your next mailing.

Writing the Second Sales *Letter*

You should write your second sales letter about three weeks after your first mailing. If you received good results with your first letter, you will need to make only minor adjustments. If the results were poor, you may have to make major alterations. You should not hesitate to do this. The factor that distinguishes good from poor results is not replies, but interviews. You should plan on about two days to write a new sales letter.

Printing the Letterheads and Envelopes for Your Second Letter

If you planned ahead and had extra letterheads and envelopes printed at first, you may not need to do this. But if you did, don't hesitate to make an additional investment.

Mailing the Second Letter

You will not need to spend a lot of time compiling a new mailing list, since day-to-day record keeping has updated your initial list. Eliminate those companies on your list that have contacted you to set up an interview. Keep track of your second sales letter results, as you did your first, in case an additional mailing is required.

Setting Up Interviews

You will begin to set up interviews generated by sales letters about three weeks after your first mailing. Invitations will come from the executive you have sent the sales letter to as well as from human resources people and other staff personnel. The majority of invitations will come by telephone. This is one reason that practicing with a telephone is so important. Most executives will want to talk with you by phone before seeing you, especially if the interview requires travel at the PE's expense. Responses to faxes and e-mail letters will come much sooner.

You should continue to set up interviews until you get and accept a great job offer. You can always cancel an interview. It is much more difficult to arrange an interview after you have told a PE that you are declining because you expect a job offer. You may then have to answer embarrassing questions about why the offer was not extended. Of course, after you interview and have made a "sale," you are free to say you are expecting another offer or have received one.

Certain other alternative ways of getting interviews may be important to your campaign and should be integrated into your overall campaign plan.

● THE INTERVIEW PHASE OF YOUR CAMPAIGN

Preparing for the Interview

Once you have an interview lined up, you should learn everything possible about the hiring executive, the company, and its products. You should also develop a list of questions to ask and prep yourself for questions that are likely to be asked of you. Plan on several hours of preparation for each face-to-face interview that you schedule. One successful candidate I worked with spent two weeks in preparation. It resulted in an $240,000 a year offer in today's dollars. This was more than a 100 percent increase over his former salary when he was working—and he was out of work at the time. I'll explain everything you need to know in Chapter 10.

Accept every interview offered, unless you are offered so many that time forces you to pick and choose. And by the way, that has happened to many who have employed these methods.

One of my students couldn't get a single interview. After he stopped sending out resumes to human resource departments and started sending sales letters to decision-makers, he wrote that he had to start turning interviews down.

Even if you are pressed for time, you should try to make every single interview you can. Schedule two interviews or more a day if you have to. Remember, interviews and interviews alone will get you job offers. Also, if you apply yourself, you will get better with every interview. By the end of your campaign you will be getting job offers you would not have received when you first started interviewing. Finally, you will learn more about the job and whether you really want it from the interview than from any other source (short of actually working for the company).

● THE POSTINTERVIEW PHASE OF YOUR CAMPAIGN

Writing the Follow-up Sales Letter

The follow-up sales letter is written and mailed within a day after the interview. Plan on spending several hours getting this letter just right. Unless you are one of the lucky job hunters who are deluged by interviews, you should have no problem getting an outstanding follow-up sales letter written and mailed promptly. I will show you how to write this letter in Chapter 13.

Preparing the Special Resume

The special resume is generally prepared after the interview and can be mailed with the follow-up sales letter. In a few cases, generally if the PE must pay your travel expenses, you may have to send out a special resume before the interview. In this case, you will use techniques I will teach you elsewhere in the book to obtain all the intelligence you can about the position and to base your special resume on this information. It should take you no more than a couple of hours to prepare a special resume, since you have already assembled all the facts and materials you need at the beginning of your campaign.

Negotiating

Negotiations can take much longer than you might imagine. And you must always negotiate. I'll explain why and tell you how to negotiate in Chapter 14.

This is especially true in large companies or companies that have several different executives involved in the decision-making process. As much as three weeks can elapse between the time that you and the hiring executive come to a meeting of the minds and the time that you receive an offer.

● THE TEN-WEEK CAMPAIGN AND HOW TO SHORTEN IT

It is difficult to describe the length of an "average" campaign, because there is no such thing. Every job hunter has his own objectives which he has defined, and every individual's situation is different. However, in very general terms, the campaign detailed in this chapter is designed to last approximately ten weeks, from start to acceptance of the offer. This allows extra time for consideration of the offer, delays by the PE, and administrative tasks such as printing and typing. You can shorten the ten-week campaign by reducing the time for subcontracted tasks such as printing, having someone else do your typing, or working more than eight hours a day on your campaign. Another way to shorten the time is not to set excessively high requirements as part of your job objective.

If you are currently employed or in school, you will not be able to spend eight hours a day on your campaign. If you are employed, you may need to campaign in secret. You must work harder than the unemployed executive. Work hard on your campaign at night and on weekends. Get someone else to do your typing. Unless you can take a vacation, you will not be able to work on the telephone. Also, you may have difficulty setting up interviews or meetings with employment agencies.

Figure 1-1 represents a completed campaign plan for an unemployed job hunter who is not campaigning in secret and who is putting in eight hours every day plus weekends on the campaign. Figure 1-2 is a completed campaign plan for an employed job hunter campaigning in secret. It assumes that someone else does typing and that interviews will be scheduled for after hours or on weekends. Using these two examples, design your own job campaign plan. Figure 1-3 is a blank campaign form to enable you to do so.

Once you have put your campaign plan into action, you will need to adjust your plan. Certain tasks may take you less time than you planned; other tasks may take longer or may have to be repeated. In addition, responses to your sales letters and answers to advertisements will not all arrive at the same time. You may receive an offer from one company at the same time as your interview with another company. You should adjust your plan accordingly. Finally, you may find yourself so successful in some phase of your campaign (for example, getting

WEEK	1	2	3	4	5	6	7	8	9	10	PHASE
Prepare resume	↑										I
Write initial sales letters		↑									
Set up number to receive telephone calls		↑									
Set up address to receive letters		↑									
Print initial sales letters			↑								
Develop mailing lists			↑								
Type addresses and mail sales letters			↑								
Break "blind" advertisements							↑				
Answer advertisements								↑			
Employments agency interviews							↑				
Talk to friends							↑				
Write second sales letters						↑					
Print second sales letters							↑				
Type addresses and mail second sales letters								↑			
Set up interviews									↑		
Interviews									↑		
Write and send postinterview letter/resume									↑		II
Negotiations										↑	
Offer acceptance										↑	III

Figure 1-1. Campaign plan for an employed job hunter.

WEEK	1	2	3	4	5	6	7	8	9	10	PHASE
											I II III
Prepare resume	↑										
Write initial sales letters	↑										
Print initial sales letters		↑									
Develop mailing lists		↑									
Type addresses and mail sales letters		↑									
Answer advertisements								↑			
Telephone training program					↑						
Employment agency interviews					↑						
Talk to friends					↑						
Write second sales letters					↑						
Print second sales letters							↑				
Type addresses and mail second sales letters						↑					
Set up interviews									↑		
Interviews									↑		
Write and send postinterview letter/resume										↑	
Negotiations										↑	
Offer acceptance										↑	

Figure 1-2. Campaign plan for an unemployed job hunter.

PHASE

WEEK	1	2	3	4	5	6	7	8	9	10

Figure 1-3. Your job campaign plan.

more interviews than you can handle) that good sense dictates holding other campaign tasks in abeyance.

The Main Point

Start your campaign for a new job on your first day of work at the old job and don't fool around. Job seeking for a great job is serious stuff: It must be conducted through a planned campaign.

**MAKE THE RESUME
THE FOUNDATION
OF YOUR CAMPAIGN**

2

How to Prepare the Foundation: Your Mind

"I just had to send you this e-mail to thank you. I worked in an engineering department as a controls programmer. A corporate decision was made to eliminate my position and I was laid off after twelve years. It took me approximately ten weeks, but after studying and applying your techniques, I was able to attain a similar position with another company and increased my gross salary by 45%. Of course this was without a resume. And can you believe it, now my old firm wants me back at an even higher increase. Thank you, Dr. Cohen."

—An Enthusiastic Supporter

You may not like the "touchie-feelie" stuff. It makes no difference; if you want a great job fast, you must first attain the goal of that job in your mind. No great anything was ever achieved until someone did this. The motto of The Royal Air Force goes something along the lines that "what man can conceive, he can achieve." And that's absolutely true. But the converse is also true. If you cannot conceive of yourself getting a great job, you will not be able to do so. To start conceiving the great job in your mind, you must start with a positive mental attitude.

● HOW TO GET A POSITIVE MENTAL ATTITUDE

Whether you are currently unemployed, not yet in your first job, or secure in your job, a positive mental attitude is crucial. Your mental attitude will make a difference in how soon you find a job, what kind of job you are offered and accept, and how much compensation you receive. Even if you follow all the advanced techniques explained in breaking the rules, you will be wasting your time in job interviews unless you have the right mental attitude. But if you enter every interview with a positive attitude, you will receive job offers that you never dreamed possible.

Now some of you reading this will say, "I'm not interested in any mental attitude hocus pocus." Before you make up your mind, let me tell you about George Y., a petroleum engineer whose positive mental attitude got him a job offer when there wasn't even an opening. Through various techniques that I will explain in later chapters, George was able to speak on the phone to the divisional vice president of a large, independent petroleum producer.

The vice president, impressed by George's positive personality and attitude, invited him in for a talk, even though "the only opening we have now is for a geologist."

George maintained his positive mental attitude throughout a long interview. Two weeks later he was invited back to "meet some of our people." Not once was a job mentioned, and not once did George ask. But he maintained his positive attitude and demonstrated his natural enthusiasm for petroleum work and his interest in the company he was "visiting." Several days later George received a job offer. The company had decided that it needed a petroleum engineer more than it needed a geologist. What really happened, of course, was that management decided that a positive fellow like George was too good to pass up.

● BE PREPARED FOR THE INEVITABLE SETBACKS

No matter how good you are or what you have done in the past, you are going to suffer some hard knocks during your campaign. Not all prospective employers (PEs) are going to like you, appreciate your talents, or understand your accomplishments, just as you are not going to like or appreciate every PE you meet. Sometime during your campaign you will meet a PE whom you like very much. You will think yourself a perfect match for the company and feel that you will be able to do wonders for it. You will be disappointed if you do not receive a job offer. Unfortunately, that is exactly what is going to happen. You will not receive one. Why? Who knows? There are ten thousand reasons that may have nothing to do with you. In fact, they may actually want to offer you the job, but cannot. Maybe the president's son or daughter decided he or she wanted the job. Maybe there was a full moon out. Who knows? The reasons are unimportant. What is important is that you be ready for such temporary setbacks. Like a good marriage, the perfect job match comes when both parties are totally convinced and all the other unimportant, weird, and random factors fall into line as well. In the interim you must maintain your positive mental attitude. Eventually they will. Meanwhile, here's how to keep positive.

After a terrific interview that you are certain will lead to an offer, get ready for the next interview with the next company anyway. Tell yourself that you are going to have such a great "next" interview that you will receive another offer to compare against the one you expect. Then answer additional advertisements, as explained in Chapter 8. See if you can raise your response-to-interview ratio by writing the "perfect" response. Make more telephone calls, following the telephone training program discussed in Chapter 9. Try to beat your old record of number of calls to interviews. If it fits in with your campaign plan, send out additional sales letters or follow-up sales letters. Go over your old letter to polish it further. Finally, be confident that in the end you will achieve your objective and capture a truly great job, whether it is with the terrific company you have just interviewed with and from which you expect a job offer, or an even better one.

● HOW TO USE YOUR RESUME TO DEVELOP A POSITIVE ATTITUDE

Even after you have developed a superior resume (which, as I will explain in Chapter 5, you will *not* be sending to PEs) and are well into your job campaign, you are not done with it. You should read over your resume every morning and evening.

There are two reasons for rereading your resume as your campaign progresses. First, as your campaign develops and you begin to interview, things that you accomplished which you have forgotten will be remembered. Other accomplishments that you thought were unimportant will turn out to be very important. You will want to include the first, and perhaps reemphasize the second in your resume. Moreover, by repeatedly reading about your strong experiences, background, and most of all, accomplishments you will realize just what a tremendous "catch" you are. You really have a lot to offer. You are unique! You have a unique set of qualifications stemming from years of work or service at any number of vocations and avocations. As you reread your accomplishments, you will realize that by finding a great job, you will be rendering a service not only to yourself, but also to that organization fortunate enough to hire you. This knowledge will assist you in maintaining a positive mental attitude as you attend to everyday tasks and will actually assist you in getting that superior position sooner. Your big problem may be not being arrogant about what a fantastic job candidate you are.

● HOW TO AVOID NEGATIVE FEELINGS DURING INTERVIEWS

The only way to avoid negative feelings during interviews is to maintain positive ones. Before you interview, get to know both yourself and your PE. Find out everything you can about the job, the company, and the people you will meet. Think about how you would act in the job. Imagine yourself in the environment of that company. Picture yourself as an employee there. The more you know about the company and the more you can imagine yourself working there, the less nervous you will be and the more positive an image you will project.

During your first few interviews you may still feel some nervousness. Don't worry about it. It will lessen with time. During the next few interviews you will find yourself improving your interviewing skill. You will get better and better. In fact, many job hunters end up enjoying interviewing so much that they miss it once they have accepted a position. They enjoy interviewing because it gives them a chance to show off "people skills" they have developed and perfected. It also gives them an opportunity to meet new people in their profession and to learn about their industry and specialty. Above all, many job-hunters enjoy the challenge of interviewing, of trying to get a PE to make them a job offer.

You may not believe it now, but you too may enjoy interviewing. In fact, you may like it too much. So a word of caution: Never become so overconfident or cocky in your interviews that you lose sight of your main purpose—to get a great job.

● THE SECRET OF ALWAYS DEALING FROM STRENGTH

On several occasions when I was in industry, I resigned from one job before beginning to search for another. But I never accepted a new job without a significant salary increase. One PE even commented during an interview: "Bill, I know you are unemployed, yet you act as if you had a million dollars. What's your secret?" My secret, which enabled me to deal from strength under any circumstances, was this: I knew my own strengths. I spent a considerable amount of time working on my resume, making sure I wrote down every useful and appropriate bit of experience in my background. Knowing my strengths and remembering my accomplishments gave me tremendous self-confidence. I knew that I was a unique individual who had much to offer to the company that hired me. I also knew my job goal. I knew exactly what position I wanted, the industry, the kind of company, the location, and the compensation. Because I knew my own strengths and experience, I was confident that I could do an outstanding job in the position I decided upon.

When I was a job hunter, I knew the company or organization I was interviewing with. I studied the company's history, products, and financial position. I knew the backgrounds of some of the leading executives, including, if possible, the executive or executives with whom I interviewed. In most cases I even knew why this company was seeking my services. I made it my business to learn as much as I could before the interview. As a result, I sometimes knew as much about the company, in a general way, as the executive who was doing the interviewing.

Finally, I knew what the outcome of my campaign would be. I have seen many other executives, professionals, managers, and students find terrific jobs. I knew that I was at least as good in my own field and was confident of my ability to find a great job, myself. I knew that in some way I was superior to all other job seekers for the same job . . . to all of my competitors.

I don't know whether you are confident right now or not. I do know that in your field of choice you, too, are superior over all of your competitors in some way. I know this from many years' experience. I have never met a man or woman that I am not superior to in some way. However, I never met a man or woman who wasn't superior to me in some way, too. I know that the same is true of you.

By the time you complete this book, you will be as confident as I was.

How Ray S. Got a Great Job Through a Positive Mental Attitude

Ray S. was a young Air Force officer. He completed his service and sought a job as an engineer with an aircraft company. Ray considered his own background. He had a bachelor's degree in engineering from a respectable school. He had four years' experience as an engineer in the Air Force, where he had performed as a project manager and was responsible for the development of aircraft subsystems exceeding a million dollars per year. Ray had done very well in directing these government programs and had been commended by his supervisor.

Before beginning his campaign, Ray wrote down everything he had done during this period; after a few days he had several pages of notes. By this time he really knew his strengths. Next, Ray began to think about his goal. He knew he wanted to work for an aircraft company. Because his background was entirely in project management, and because he both enjoyed and excelled at this type of work, Ray decided to pursue it as a career. He began to investigate several aerospace companies. He discovered very quickly that his limited experience made it difficult to move into the kind of job he wanted, given the business climate of the aerospace industry at that time.

Ray did not give up. He learned of a company in a foreign country that was seeking American expertise in building up its aerospace capabilities. The company offered the type of position he sought at a higher salary than he had expected. Ray now had a fully defined job goal. To prepare himself, he studied the company and read up on the country. By the day of the interview Ray was ready. He knew that his campaign would be successful whether this particular company hired him or not. He also knew that he would do well in the interview. He was self-confident and had a positive mental attitude.

It is not remarkable that Ray S. was hired. What is remarkable is that he managed to secure a position at a level higher than 80 percent of the other American engineers who were hired, despite the fact that they had from 2 to 25 years more experience than Ray.

● YOUR ABILITY TO SELL YOURSELF THROUGH YOUR ATTITUDE

Job hunting is a sales situation. You are the product. Your PE is your customer. Other job hunters seeking the same job are your competition. In this book you will understand why breaking the rules is necessary. But in addition, you will find every tool you need to satisfy your customer and beat the competition. But these tools will be of no value unless you have a positive mental attitude as a foundation. Have you ever seen a successful salesman with a negative attitude? Of course not. The same is true for the successful job hunter. A positive mental attitude will attract job offers. A negative mental attitude expressing negative feelings or telling hard-luck stories to a PE will get you only the least desirable jobs, if any. Like the successful salesman, you should always fill your mind with positive thoughts. A positive mental attitude is the key to selling yourself successfully to a PE.

● MAINTAINING A POSITIVE OUTLOOK

Psychologists tell us that you cannot be in a happy mood and an unhappy mood at the same time. If you think about this, it makes sense. You really can't act sad when you feel happy and visa versa. If fact, if you want, you can try this right now and see that it is true. So if you want to be happy, even in the face of misery about you, it is within your own power.

For most people, just changing their posture and facial expression can have a strong therapeutic effect. Try this. If you are feeling "down" right now, sit or stand up straight, hold your head high, with your shoulders back. Now put a smile on your face. You will feel better.

Paul Ekman, professor of psychology at the University of California found that moods could be changed by simply assuming a happy face or a sad face. Students who assumed a sad face felt sad. Those who put on a happy face felt happy.[1]

To top things off, try repeating this litany at the same time: "I feel happy, I feel healthy, I feel terrific!" Keep saying this loudly and with enthusiasm until you really "feel it." W. Clements Stone of Chicago used this positive affirmation. He claimed it helped him maintain a positive mood under adversity. Friends and employees said Stone was a "reverse paranoid." According to Stone, others were constantly plotting to do good things for him. Maybe he was correct. Though born poor, he became a millionaire many times over.

Here's another little experiment you can try right now. Try to feel really bad when you are in the "happy posture" with a big smile. If you have nothing to smile about right now, think of when you did. What has been your biggest success in life so far? It doesn't matter if it was a really big victory or not. Think how you felt when you achieved that success or received some very good news. Did it make you happy? You probably had a very big smile. Assume the same posture, facial expressions, and feelings you had when you were happy and successful in the past. Now maintaining the facial expressions, and posture of happiness, try to get depressed. Unless you change your posture, expressions, and thoughts, it just isn't possible.

You may be interested to know that nature may have a sound explanation for this phenomenon. When we smile or frown, muscles tighten to compress small blood vessels from the carotid artery. This regulates the volume of blood supplied to the brain. So key regions of the brain get more or less blood and more or less of the mood-altering chemicals in the blood. According to psychologist R. B. Zajonc at the University of Michigan, nature may have intended that people control their emotions in this way. [2]

This simple mood control exercise has considerable power. How do you feel when you are in a happy mood? Most people feel "charged up." They feel unbeatable. They feel that all is "right with the world." They feel they can't do anything wrong. They are "on a roll." This can have an amazing affect on how you proceed and how you are perceived as you meet potential employers during your campaign.

● SOLVING PROBLEMS THAT OCCUR DURING YOUR CAMPAIGN

Here's another psychological technique that will improve your ability to solve problems as they occur. It is a form of self-hypnosis and was developed by researchers at Duke University. First, you select the major problem bothering you. Next, you go off by yourself where it is quiet. Sit down and allow yourself to relax, with your eyes closed. Most people find they can get in such a relaxed state by slowly imagining numbness spreading over their bodies beginning with their toes, and not even excluding their eyelids.

While in this relaxed state, you simply describe the problem to yourself in your mind and tell your subconscious mind that you want the problem solved. You then get up and go about your business. Not infrequently, the results are almost immediate and the solution will come to you when you least expect it. Sometimes the problem is solved a little later with the solution appearing in different or unexpected ways. Repeat the procedure periodically until the problem is solved to your satisfaction.

I know this sounds too good and too simple to be true. But it has been tested and found to work. During experiments testing this technique, one hundred and fifty-five college students tried it on a wide variety of problems. Eighty-six percent of the students reported complete or partial success at helping or preventing depression; 94.9 percent reported complete or partial success at becoming wide awake when sleepy; 97.2 percent reported complete or partial success at overcoming fatigue; 91.9 percent reported complete or partial success at curing procrastination; and 98.7 percent reported complete or partial success at improving their social relations.[3] Many executives and students I have worked with report similar success with a wide variety of business and personal problems.

● USING THE BODY'S CHEMICAL SYSTEM TO CHANGE YOUR MENTAL ATTITUDE

In his book, *Anatomy of an Illness,* Norman Cousins explained how he saved his life through his own body's chemistry. Afterwards, Cousins, although not trained as a medical doctor, served as an adjunct professor at UCLA's School of Medicine. Speaking at California State University Los Angeles' graduation several years ago, he theorized that the human body contains its own drugs which can cause physiological, as well as psychological, change to cure any disease. These chemicals are released through specific psychological or physical stimulation that we don't fully understand yet.

One of the most powerful of these drugs are those classed as *endorphins*. Strenuous exercise can release endorphins. That is probably the explanation for the euphoria frequently experienced by joggers toward the end of a workout and known as a "runner's high." So maintaining a consistent exercise regime is one way of ensuring endorphins are in your bloodstream on a regular basis.

However, you don't need to exercise to release endorphins. Cousins was able to release endorphins while on his "deathbed" by securing a large quantity of video tapes starring his favorite comedians, "The Three Stooges," and playing them nonstop. At first, the going was tough. He found that six hours of belly laughs would release sufficient endorphins to allow him fifteen minutes of sleep. Slowly, the endorphins worked their magic and eventually he was able to get the sleep he needed for recovery.

I have helped train thousands of executives and students in seminars on how to release endorphins by a simple exercise. I ask the executives to stand, close their eyes, and allow their minds and bodies to relax.

I then ask them to imagine that when they return home that evening they will find a registered letter among their mail. The letter is from an attorney. The attorney explains that an uncle whom they never knew has passed away. This uncle was extremely wealthy. As a final gift to his long lost niece or nephew, he has left the sum of $1,000,000, tax free, which is enclosed. The only condition is that they must spend this money in any way they wish. They can buy a home or an expensive car. They can take a trip around the world, or buy a boat. They can give the money to their church, synagogue or a favorite charity. Or they can do some combination of these or other things.

I give the executives several minutes to imagine their good fortune and the wonderful things they can immediately do with this tax-free money. I then tell them that on the count of three I want them to open their eyes and within ten seconds tell two other executives of their good fortune and what they are going to do with the money. They are to do this in the most excited way they can. And why not, wouldn't you be excited if you had just been given a million dollars, tax-free to do anything you want with today?

You can actually feel the excitement building as I count slowly "one . . . two . . . THREE!" The room breaks out into a loud babble of noise. After ten seconds I stop these executives—not always easily. I invite them to feel the endorphins coursing through their veins. All agree that they feel fantastic.

Now you can do the same exercise by yourself. Also, you don't have to imagine a rich uncle keeps leaving you one million dollars. You can imagine anything else that pleases you and makes you happy.

You might try this. Pick your dream. Sit back and daydream. Imagine you have achieved one or more of your dreams, whatever they are: financial, personal, job related or not. Think about what things will be like. Imagine enjoying your success. Really give yourself a squirt of endorphins. Dose yourself with a "dream session" daily. Many job hunters tell me they eventually achieve the great job they think about after releasing endorphins in this way. Remember, what we can conceive, we can achieve.

● "ANCHORING" TECHNIQUES

"Anchoring" is one of the many neuro-linguistic programming techniques developed by Professor John Grinder and his student, Richard Bandler, at the University of California, Santa Cruz back in the 1970s. These scientists discovered that emotions could become linked to physical actions or sensations. For example, if while you were in an intensely depressed mood, a number of people attempted to console you by squeezing your left shoulder, depression could be brought on months or even years later by the simple act of someone squeezing the same shoulder in the same way.

This is an unplanned anchor. However, you can also set an intentional anchor yourself. Maybe you recall the famous experiment of Dr. Pavlov. Dr. Pavlov rang a bell whenever he brought food to his dog. His dog, of course, would salivate. After awhile, Dr. Pavlov didn't need the food to get his dog to salivate. All he needed to do was to ring the bell. The emotion and sensations of hunger were now linked to the bell.

You can use anchoring on yourself to get any emotion you want on demand. Let's say you want to feel strong. Think of a time when you felt particularly strong in the past. In your mind's eye, review everything that occurred. See everything as it happened, hear the sounds, smell the smells . . . everything.

What you are trying to do is to get yourself in an intense state of the same emotion. As you feel yourself in this intense state, take some unique physical action such as squeezing your hand into a fist. That action is similar to Dr. Pavlov's action in ringing a bell.

As soon as you do this once, repeat the sequence. Keep repeating it. After awhile, you will have anchored the squeezing of your fist to the emotion of strength. Whenever you squeeze your fist, you will feel strong.

You can do this with any feeling you want to generate at that time: happiness, calmness, strength . . . whatever you want!

Of course, you must use a different "bell" for each different emotion. That is, pull different fingers, squeeze your wrist, and so on.

You can imagine how valuable a technique this is. Let's say that you get nervous during an interview. All you need to do is to take the action to initiate your anchor to feel calm.

Don't forget to pick something unique and different for each anchor. Otherwise, either you or someone else can accidentally trigger an emotion that you might not desire at that particular time.

If not triggered, some anchors will expire on their own over time. If you want to intentionally erase an unwanted anchor, trigger a stronger anchor to a different emotion simultaneously with the one you want to erase. The stronger anchor will erase the weaker one.

The Main Point

You can control your emotions. You can be as happy and positive as you want to be. And you can use these mental techniques to help you to get a great job fast. Your mind is the real foundation of any job campaign.

● NOTES

1. David Lewis, *The Secret Language of Success* (New York: Carroll & Graf Publishers, Inc., 1989), p. 68.
2. *Op. Cit.,* p. 67.
3. Dr. Hornell Hart, *Autoconditioning* (New York: Prentice-Hall, 1975), p. 248.

LEAVE ALL YOUR OPTIONS OPEN

3

WHY YOU MUST DECIDE WHAT YOU WANT AND FOCUS ON A SINGLE JOB OPTION

"Your guidance was a Godsend because I had been laid off for about six months and wanted to get a great job fast! After working for a Big Six accounting firm for fourteen years, I decided to leave accounting and focus on a job as a marketing manager. Many people doubted that I could find a marketing job that could compete with what I had before in terms of salary and benefits. But I did. And in my new job that I start next week, I have the opportunity to become marketing director."

—New Marketing Manager

Most "experts" tell us to complete a resume in which you state a general career or job objective, not a specific job by title. That way, they tell us, all our options will be left open and we will be surprised at the wonderful opportunities that will be presented to us, that we may never have thought of.

Let me tell you emphatically that this rule is 100% wrong and will only result in a delay in your getting interviews that will lead to a great job. Why? There are several reasons for this:

- A prospective employer is not interested in helping you decide on your career choice.
- Your image or positioning as the most qualified candidate for a particular job will be diluted.
- The basis of all competitive strategy is concentration of superior resources at the decisive point.

Let's look at each of these in turn and find out why it is so critical to focus on a single job option.

● A PROSPECTIVE EMPLOYER IS NOT INTERESTED IN HELPING YOU DECIDE ON YOUR CAREER CHOICE

Yes, that's the hard fact of life. A prospective employer has a problem that needs solving. As your prospective employer sees it, the person who will help him to solve that problem is an expert, a specialist who has a specific set of skills. He's happy that you have a career objective of "joining a company where you can make the greatest contribution" or "developing your abilities to maximum potential." But that does nothing for him. A prospective employer is not a friend, relative, career counselor, rabbi, priest, or minister. Your prospective employer isn't responsible for figuring out where you best fit or can "make the biggest contribution." He expects you to figure that out and tell that to him. He doesn't have the time to do your work for you.

● YOUR IMAGE OR POSITIONING AS THE MOST QUALIFIED FOR A PARTICULAR JOB WILL BE DILUTED

Some years ago, two advertising experts, Al Ries and Jack Trout, wrote a book entitled *Positioning* (McGraw-Hill, 1981) which set the marketing world on its ear. In the book, they developed their concept of positioning. It has since become a cornerstone of basic marketing theory.

What Trout and Ries postulated was that a marketer of any product or service (and as a job seeker selling yourself, that's you, right?) must strive to create a specific and distinct position relative to his competition in the mind of prospective buyers. Moreover, this position should target a market with laser precision. Any attempt to be everything to everybody, and thus expand their market, would only result in disaster. They gave example after example of well-known firms that fell exactly into that trap.

Cadillac once held the position as the number one luxury car in the country. It was also the most expensive. When you wanted to say something was the very best, you said "Cadillac." Up and comers aspired to one day own a Cadillac. Then some bright young "genius" at General Motors came up with the idea of expanding the market for Cadillac by creating a smaller, less expensive model. The idea was that then a lot more people could afford and would want a Cadillac, and would therefore buy the car. So, Cadillac came up with the Seville. And Cadillac sold a bundle. The only problem is, it cost Cadillac its position as the number one luxury car.

As Trout and Ries noted, someone forgot about what happened to the Packard Company earlier. Packard was the premier American car before World War II, and was a status symbol all over the world. You guessed it, Packard tried the same stunt with a relatively inexpensive model called the Packard Clipper. It was the most successful car Packard ever built. The only problem was it killed Packard's positioning and by 1954, killed the company.

Now we aren't talking about cars, but the concept of positioning holds true. You want to be one laser-focused master of whatever it is you do, or want to do, to your prospective employer. Don't end up with fuzzy positioning by trying to be everything to everybody with one of those "one size fits all" job objectives without one single, specific, job in mind.

● THE BASIS OF ALL COMPETITIVE STRATEGY IS CONCENTRATION OF SUPERIOR RESOURCES AT THE DECISIVE POINT

When you are in a campaign to get a great job fast, you are in a competition with thousands of other job seekers who are looking for exactly the same job. Each of these job seeker-competitors has limited resources, limited money to spend, limited personal time, and limited time or space to make a presentation to a prospective employer with which to convince him that he or she is one of the top candidates who should be seen in an interview.

Let's analyze this last point. There may be a hundred, or several hundred to a thousand job candidates who apply for a really great job. Every competitor is doing his or her best to convince the prospective employer that he or she is the best candidate for that particular job.

Let's pick a job. Let's say we are competing for a really great job as a financial analyst. Although resumes are a poor way to convince anyone that we are the best financial analyst (and as I promised, I will show you why in Chapter 5), let's assume for the sake of our analysis that we'll use a resume in this case. Moreover, we'll assume that every competitor is limited to a two page resume, with the identical font size, and the spacing the same.

Most competitors will submit a standard resume of experiences. Some of these experiences or accomplishments will support the job seeker's case as being best candidate for this particular job, but others will not. For example, it is quite an accomplishment to speak thirty-two dialects of a "dead" language spoken in ancient China, but since this accomplishment has nothing to do with expertise as a financial analyst, it is wasted space on this two-page resume.

On the other hand, if you concentrate whatever financial analytical background and accomplishments you have in this two-page resume, you will appear much stronger to your prospective employer than a competitor who does not do this. That's an example of concentrating superior resources at the decisive point. The results will hold true even when competitors have more experience as financial analysts, but try to show expertise in other fields on this same two-page resume.

This is so important, I want to repeat it. When you concentrate all your resources against the decisive point represented by a specific job, you will be stronger than candidates who do not do this, even if a competitor has done more, but fails to concentrate by talking about accomplishments not directly relevant to the target job.

● YOU CAN'T GET A JOB UNTIL YOU KNOW THE JOB YOU WANT

Many job hunters start their campaigns with only the fuzziest notion of the kind of job they want. Some think this is an advantage: If they keep "all their options open," they might get a job that they would otherwise have overlooked. Don't make this mistake! True, as your campaign progresses your job goal will become clearer. But you can lose job offers if you aren't specific about the job you seek, right from the start.

PEs are interested in men and women who know their own minds and know what they want in life. They are much less interested in suggesting opportunities to you or trying to help you find something of interest on the remote possibility that you might be qualified. Further, PEs are interested in you because of expertise you are offering in an area which they feel they are currently lacking. This might be in sales, it might be in finance, or it might be in general management. Anything you say that does not reinforce your image as the best candidate for the job will work to your disadvantage. Even if you speak ten languages, this skill will only blur your image if it is not directly related to the position you are seeking. Further, in a job campaign, *time*—your most important resource—is limited. To be successful, you must concentrate your efforts on developing a single well-defined opportunity. You cannot afford to dissipate your energies by going after many different job goals simultaneously.

Finally, you cannot plan steps toward reaching a job goal until you decide exactly what that job goal is. There is one exception to this rule. Despite the fact that you have aimed at a single type of job and have prepared your job campaign accordingly, occasionally a PE will single out an accomplishment in your resume and ask whether you would be interested in a position other than the one you are seeking. You will have to evaluate such an opportunity on its own merits. Even so, you should never establish more than one precisely defined goal at the start or allow a singular interest by one PE to redirect your entire job campaign. In short, spend some time deciding what you want, then go after that specific goal.

● WHY YOU MUST ESTABLISH YOUR OVERALL CAREER GOAL

If you are like many, your next job is not the last job you will hold. It is one more milestone in your career. Before you can establish a milestone goal, you must establish an overall career goal. Each person's professional career goal will differ. A company president may aspire to be president of a much larger company, president of a company in another industry, or to start his or her own business. Anyone may even want to leave industry entirely and go into something else.

Regardless of your current or planned function or job level, you must establish an overall professional career goal. Once you do, you can begin thinking about what jobs you must have as milestones in order to achieve your overall career goal. Then you can focus on the job you want as your next intermediate goal and concentrate your resources on attaining it.

Many unemployed job hunters think that they can easily get a job if only they take a step down. This is a mistake. In fact, it is generally easier to take another step up than to go backward. If you try to get a job on a lower level or for less money, your PE will feel that there must be something wrong and will assume that if you have once worked at a higher level you will not be happy working at a lower one. Further, your PE will be afraid that you will leave the first time you are offered a job at your proper level. The same is true if you are a new graduate, willing to accept a position that does not require a college degree.

Going backward is an uphill battle. It is a battle you should not fight. You should always seek a job that builds on what you have done before, so that your career proceeds in a logical sequence. If you have not done this in the past, the time to start is now.

● THE EASIEST JOB TO GET

What type of job is the easiest to get? The easiest job to get is one in your present industry, in an identical or similar function to the one you now perform, and in the same or a similar-size company. It is a job at the same level as or one level higher than the one at which you are now working, at a salary 10 to 20 percent higher than what you are presently earning. For a quick and relatively easy job hunt, you must take these five factors into consideration. A sixth factor, geographical location, you may or may not want to consider in your job-hunting campaign. If you are a student, it is the kind of job other students are getting . . . but you'll be able to get a better quality job of the same kind faster than others using the techniques in this book.

This does not mean that you cannot immediately increase your present salary by 25 percent or more, change industries or functions, go from a large company to a small one (or vice versa), move to a desirable geographical location, or jump several levels in responsibility. However, if any or all of these objectives are part of your job goal, you should recognize that they will make your search more difficult than "the easiest job to get." You will have to allow for a longer and more difficult campaign. Of course, if you are willing to put in this time and effort, you can do a lot better. Christina, one of my undergraduate students in marketing, attained her goal of becoming a general manager of a small company as her first job after graduation. Another undergraduate student of mine from Australia obtained a first job as an assistant product manager with a major corporation here in the United States.

● HOW TO DEFINE YOUR SPECIFIC JOB OBJECTIVES

You have established an overall professional career goal and identified job position steps that will take you there. You are now ready to precisely define the job you will be seeking, a position that will also be the next step toward reaching your overall career goal.

Industry

Do your overall career plans call for you to "make it" in the industry in which you are presently working, or must you make a change? Generally, it is easier to get a job in the industry in which you were most recently employed, even during a recession, because any industry always needs good people, even if that industry is in a recessionary mode, or maybe especially then. The only exception is if your industry is disappearing. If you were in the vinyl record business when CDs took over, the time to move was *now*. That's like being in buggy whips when buggies started to disappear. However, this is not true if you are simply in an industry that is in a temporary recession. In this case, your task is to communicate your outstanding qualifications better than your competitors. If you make an industry change during a recession, you will frequently find that much of your competition has moved with you. Unless you have prior experience in the industry or are currently employed in it, you will not have a real advantage over the competition. The same, of course, holds true even if there is no recession. Those of your competitors seeking positions in the same industry that are already working in it have the advantage.

What if your career plans give you no choice? You have decided that you need experience in another industry in order to progress, or other factors have led you to the decision to make a career outside of the industry in which you are presently employed regardless of the increased difficulty in getting a job. Then your campaign must be organized to stress your functional accomplishments, and industry should be de-emphasized. You should define exactly what industry you are going after and you should learn everything about that industry that you possibly can. If you have the time to take courses before beginning your campaign, by all means take them. Successful completion will provide additional support for an industry switch. Read all the books you can and pick up the buzzwords. Talk with friends or former classmates who are currently working in the industry. You can change industries successfully if you plan the change carefully and allow yourself additional time for your campaign.

Company

It's easier to get a position with the same type and size of company as the one you are presently working for. However, changing the type of company is easier than changing industry. Any prior experience in the type of company you are seeking will make your path much smoother, provided you use the techniques I discuss elsewhere in this book. So if you are now with a small company and have at one time been with a much larger one (or vice versa), you will probably have little trouble getting back in. If you have not had prior experience, your task will be a little more difficult.

In all your communications with potential employers, you should stress both the similarity of work and the similarity of positions. You should accentuate the positive, withholding information about major company differences until the interview, and unless asked. Before the interview you are not obligated to reveal any information about present or past employers that does not support your case. One way of doing this (and I will explain in more detail later) is simply to omit the company name from information you supply before an interview. Use descriptive terms such as "a prestigious consulting company," "a well-known finance company," "an important aerospace firm," or "one of America's leading pharmaceutical houses." If you are asked over the telephone for names, say that for security reasons you prefer to withhold this information until mutual interest has been established. Once that interest has been established, you will usually be asked to give detailed background data.

Function

Even if you have had prior experience, you should give a great deal of thought before attempting to change function. It is one of the most difficult career changes to pull off, because it raises serious questions in the mind of your PE. Why are you changing? If you have the experience and talent in the function you are seeking, why doesn't your present employer give you an opportunity in that area? However, it most definitely can be done. Murray J. moved after six years in accounting into marketing by emphasizing the marketing aspects of his accounting jobs.

If you decide to change functions, you should marshal every accomplishment and experience in your background for support. You must also be prepared to explain why you want to change. Obviously answers such as "I thought I'd give it a try" or "I want to get experience in more than one functional area so that I can break into general management" will usually kill your chances. So you must spend extra time preparing for the interview to make sure you have an argument that is reasonable and will be acceptable to your PE.

Level

Changing levels is one area where you can jump big, within certain limits. These limits are that your last job should appear to lead into the new job you are seeking. For support you can use one or more of the following:

- Salary level
- References (level and type)
- Title of individual you currently report to
- Number of people you currently supervise
- Responsibility (quantified in dollars)
- Title of your present job

You should be able to find some support in these six factors. For example, you may be able to find some high-level references (company president, congressman, high-ranking military officer) from your past. You should be able to figure out your responsibilities in dollars—the dollar value of the programs you are working on, annual sales, dollar value of the acquisitions you analyzed and recommended, or whatever. If you haven't done this before, the total value will probably amaze you. If your current title does not reflect your present responsibilities, make it so. I am not recommending that you promote yourself to a company officership. However, if your company gives a title such as "engineer" to everyone from a new hire on through the ranks, you should state your title according to the function you are actually fulfilling: project engineer, program manager, chief engineer, and so on.

What can you do if you are a student? What you shouldn't promote is your grade point average, courses taken, or specialized programs. Does that sound wrong? Believe me it isn't. As soon as you refer to these standard items, you put yourself in that large group of job seekers known collectively as "the new graduate." You will be considered along with everyone else. Normally that's bad enough. In a recession year, that's awful. What should you do? Refer to accomplishments in part-time jobs, elected positions in clubs, volunteer work, and relevant classroom work. What sort of relevant classroom work? Marketing plans, research projects, studies, case analyses all count. You'll state these as accomplishments as I'll show you in later chapters.

Do not volunteer any information that does not offer support for the job level you are seeking. That means that if you are a student, you don't need to state that your classroom accomplishments were done in the classroom. If asked, of course, answer honestly. As a rule, you should withhold exact information on references and salary until final negotiations. You can usually sidestep any other questions you would like to avoid by controlling the interview, as outlined in Chapter 10.

When you get down to final negotiations, you will have to furnish references, and you may be forced into stating your last salary. Make certain your references are of the same seniority or higher than the position you will report to. You will do nothing to help your cause if you are looking for a position in top management and offer as a reference a first-line supervisor. A cardinal rule is to avoid discussing salary at all; if you must, use the techniques outlined in Chapters 10 and 14. Make certain that your reported salary fits in with other job information you have given and is at most 20 to 30 percent lower than the anticipated salary of the position you are seeking. If you are shooting for even bigger gains, read on.

Compensation

Whether you are employed are not, it is always easier to take a jump up in salary, barring a major depression. If your goal is to make a really big jump in salary, do not tell any PE your present salary level. (The reasons are explained in detail elsewhere in this book.) You should negotiate salary on the basis of what the new position merits, not what you have made previously. Even if your goal is a moderate increase, you should follow this principle. If for any reason you are forced into revealing your former salary, be certain to include bonus, automobile, stock options, and other fringes as part of the total compensation package.

Once you have released salary information about yourself to a PE, you should recognize that you probably limited yourself to a 10 to 20 percent increase. But there are exceptions to this rule, and you are still free to try to negotiate whatever compensation you want. As a headhunter, I once watched a young oil landsman who was in great demand negotiate himself a 66 percent increase in salary. I also witnessed a much-needed professional turn down a 300 percent increase over what he had been making. In each case, the PE knew the candidate's compensation level. But these cases are exceptions to what is most definitely the norm.

Geographical Location

Geographical location, unlike the other five factors, is rarely negotiated. Still, it is an important part of your job objective, and you must give it some thought. If you are willing to go anywhere in the world to meet the other parts of your objective, that is fine. If you are not, you should decide on location before you get started. If you are after a certain location and none other, you will have to limit the target companies you select for your campaign. There is no point sending out sales letters to companies in the East when you know that you will accept a new position only in Arizona. I needn't add that certain garden spots are almost impossible to capture because of incredible competition, coupled with low demand. A little investigation at the beginning can save you much time and effort.

You won't need to bring up the subject of geographical location to your PE. Either the location will be self-evident or at some point the PE will say, "Would you consider an assignment in . . . ?" You should know the answer to this question before you begin your campaign.

After studying this chapter, sit down and decide on your job objective in terms of the factors we have discussed. Then write down a complete description of the job you want.

The Main Point

Someone who focuses on one specific job option appears to be much stronger for that job than someone who presents himself as "a jack of all trades," whether he actually is stronger or not. So, if you want a great job fast, spend the time to decide what you want and focus on a single job option.

BREAK THE RULE

APPLY TO THE HR, PERSONNEL, OR EMPLOYMENT OFFICE

4

How to Apply for a Job Directly to Your Prospective New Boss

"Much of the credit for my new job as Assistant Marketing Manager for a major corporation goes to you. Moreover, if it wasn't for your techniques, I would have low-balled my salary requirements. I would have received 33% less or possibly blown the whole offer."

—A Recent Graduate

t's a "no-brainer" that if you want a job you should apply to the human resources (HR), personnel, or employment office, right? This action may be a "no-brainer," but I'm here to tell you that unless you want a job with the HR, personnel, or employment office, this is 100% wrong. Here's why: these offices have no authority to hire you. The only authority they have is to screen you out.

● WHO REALLY MAKES THE HIRE DECISION?

There is only one person who makes the decision to hire you or not to hire you, and that is your future boss. But to have him or her make this decision, he or she has to know about you. If you apply to an HR department, you are simply setting up one more obstacle between you and the person who will actually make the hire decision, because while HR has the authority to turn you down, HR has no authority to hire you.

How a Vice President Hired a Man Two Minutes After a Personnel Manager Turned Him Down

Many years ago when I was a young executive, I met a man who finished engineering school as an electrical engineer right before World War II.

Because of the war, this man enlisted in the Army Air Corps and became a combat pilot. After the war he decided to go back to engineering. He saw an advertisement in the newspaper for electrical engineers wanted by an aerospace company. He went directly to the personnel office of the company. They had him complete one of those long application forms. These were the "bad old days," and among other information, the applicant was required to indicate his religion. This man was Jewish.

The personnel manager who reviewed his form looked it over and told him, "Sorry, but we don't hire Jews." There were no such things as nondiscrimination laws in those days, so the man left the personnel office to look for a job elsewhere.

As he came out of the personnel manager's office he bumped into a company executive. The two men instantly recognized each other. It was this man's classmate from engineering school just before the war. When the man I had met went into the Air Corps, his classmate had gone to work for this aerospace company. In five years he had become vice president of engineering.

"What are you doing here?" he asked my acquaintance.

"Looking for a job as an electrical engineer," he answered.

"Great, we need good engineers."

"But I was just told you don't hire Jews."

"Who told you that? I'm head of engineering and there is no such policy."

Much to the vice president's chagrin, he discovered that while he had no discriminatory policies, his personnel manager had routinely screened out all Jewish applicants. He had made it his policy. He didn't think that they wanted Jewish employees.

I tell you this story not as a commentary on the sad state of discrimination in some companies fifty years ago, but to illustrate the type of power wielded by HR. Nowadays, it is not that HR managers are "bad guys." Most are very conscientious and doing their jobs to the best of their abilities. They do the very best they can to provide the best fit and the best candidates to a decision-maker for a particular job as they understand what this individual wants. They reject all other applicants. The problem is, only the decision-maker knows exactly what he wants or does not want in a new employee for a particular job. So at the very best, going to HR will mean a delay in getting an interview. Worse, you may get screened out of a job when your prospective new boss would have preferred you to all others.

● HOW I ALMOST BECAME A VICE PRESIDENT OF A MAJOR CORPORATION WHILE STILL IN MY EARLY THIRTIES

Another real advantage of going directly to the decision-maker is that very frequently, you'll cut out a lot of competitors.

Before I got my PhD and became a professor, I was in industry. Once during one of my job campaigns, I wondered whether I could immediately move into the top ranks of a major corporation. I wrote to a number of prospective employers at only slightly higher than the job level I was seeking. However, I also wrote to a number of presidents of top corporations, seeking a job as vice president of marketing. From the latter, I got only rejects. Finally I accepted a position at slightly higher than my present level.

A week after accepting a position, I got a desperate call from a president of a major corporation on the East Coast. I lived on the West Coast. "How soon could I fly out for an interview?" he wanted to know. His vice president of marketing had resigned at five o'clock the previous afternoon. They had a major multi-million dollar contract pending, and could lose everything. He had been up all night worrying, and was in the process of working out the requirements on paper to send to HR so they could advertise in *The Wall Street Journal* when he received my letter. As I will explain in the next chapter, you should never send out the ever-popular generic resume. From my letter, he thought I could handle the job.

Now I was sorely tempted. As a young man, I certainly wanted to reach the top quickly, and this would have been great. However, I have another rule. Once I have accepted a job and given my word that I was joining a company, that was it, even if I hadn't yet started work. This was exactly the situation, so turned him down. I told the anxious president that if he was this aggressive in his search for a new vice president, I was certain he would be successful.

But note, here was a situation that because I had gone directly to the decision-maker I had absolutely no competition for this great job. Moreover, my probability of getting an offer after a fly-out under these circumstances was extremely high.

● THE MAN WHO WROTE TO *TWO* PROSPECTIVE BOSSES AT THE SAME COMPANY SIMULTANEOUSLY

What can't you do when you go directly to the decision-maker? There is nothing written that will prevent you from applying for two entirely different jobs simultaneously.

A friend of mine was a senior engineering manager at a company supplying components to aerospace. His job objective involved switching to marketing for a major aerospace company. He wanted one of two jobs: vice president of marketing reporting to the president, or failing this, marketing manager reporting to a vice president of marketing. This industry was in a recession at the time, and to make the search more interesting, this manager was unemployed. He wrote two slightly different letters, both emphasizing his marketing (not engineering) expertise. One emphasized his top-level management experience. The other focused on his accomplishments in middle management.

Now, what do you do in this case about disguising the name on the letter? After all, here he was applying for a vice president's job, which meant he must write to the president. Simultaneously, he must send sales letters to the vice president of marketing at the same company. This job hunter didn't disguise his name at all, and he mailed out both types of letters at the same time.

Eventually he got the job he sought with this dual-level approach. However, one funny thing did happen to him during his campaign. He received a telephone call from the vice president of marketing of a major aerospace corporation saying that he had received his letter and inviting him to an interview. He told his wife he was interviewing with this company and left for a morning interview. The interview went quite well. Two vice presidents took him to lunch. Normally not much of a luncheon drinker, he had a double martini with his hosts. They no sooner finished their martinis when someone at another table said, "Another round for those three gentlemen over there." So our hero had another round.

By the time they left the restaurant, they were all the best of friends. As he left the plant, the vice president of marketing grasped the candidate's hand and in somewhat erratic voice due to the martinis said, "You're our kind of guy. We like you and you'll have an offer in the mail."

The job hunter got into his car and managed to drive home. His wife—who observed that her husband had been drinking, greeted him. "I thought you went to an interview at the ABC Aerospace Company," she said. When he answered that he had, she handed him a letter from the company where he had just interviewed. "Then explain this," she challenged. The letter read as follows:

Dear Mr. X:

Mr. Jones, our president, has asked me to respond to your outstanding resume (*which he never sent*) and to check our current openings against your fine background. Unfortunately, there are no openings for someone of your brilliant qualifications at the present time. However, we are putting your resume (*which he didn't send*) in our permanent file and we will contact you the minute that an opening occurs. Thank you again for thinking of us.

Sincerely,

A. W. Watkins,
Manager of Human Resources

This job hunter started laughing because, as he explained to his wife, the president of this company had been and was still in Europe enjoying a vacation. What had happened was the secretary had screened out his letter addressed to the president. She sent it to the human resources department. He had received the personnel manager's standard form-letter answer. He did get the promised offer from this company. He told me that he would have taken it except that he received a better one from another aerospace firm.

This incident illustrates just how far you can go in your job campaign. You may wonder whether, in any firm, the vice president of marketing and the president ever talked about the two different letters for different positions they received. The answer is yes. As a matter of fact, at the company that finally hired him, the president and the vice president of marketing had compared notes. What did they think? They thought it was rather clever. Maybe that's one reason he got the offer.

Now I know I may have piqued your interest regarding the sales letters that were mentioned several times. We'll get to them beginning in Chapter 5.

The Main Point

Don't go to the HR, personnel, or employment office unless you want to work for these offices. Apply for a job directly to the person who has the real hire authority: your prospective new boss.

SEND A GREAT RESUME TO PROSPECTIVE EMPLOYERS

5

THE SECRET OF GETTING A GREAT JOB WITHOUT A RESUME

"I couldn't believe it. The response was so great, I couldn't keep up with the demand for interviews. Until I followed your advice, I couldn't get a single interview, even with the help of the career development center . . . and this school cost a fortune. Then I followed your advice and quit using resumes. The results were phenomenal!"

—A Recent College Graduate

veryone knows that crafting a beautiful resume for general distribution to prospects is a "must" for getting a job. But what everyone knows is wrong. You must break this rule if you want to get a great job, fast.

● WHY YOU MUST AVOID USING A RESUME

There are several reasons why a beautifully crafted resume—or any generic resume that isn't especially prepared for a specific job at a specific company, usually prepared *after* the job interview—will fail for its intended objective. And this is true no matter how outstanding your background.

Actually many job seekers don't understand that the purpose of the resume is not to get a job offer. No one is going to hire you for a great job sight unseen and without an interview. That would be foolish on the part of any legitimate prospective employer. The purpose of a resume is to win a face-to-face interview which in turn leads to a job offer. However, most resumes won't even do that. Here's why.

The resume is an overview of your professional life and educational experience that is designed to show a prospective employer what you can do for that organization. The trouble is every company and organization is different and each has entirely different needs at different times. As a result, what you may think is important and what a prospective employer thinks is important are usually not the same.

So you have a collection of different experiences and accomplishments, some of which are important to any organization at any given time, and most of which are not. Some long-forgotten project, which you worked on for several days, may be of far more importance to a particular organization than other projects on which you may have worked for years. Chances are that a two- or three-day project is not in your resume. Until you know that company's needs better, you won't know what you've done that this company really wants to know about.

Listing a chronological work history is no help. Boiling your entire history down to one or two pages containing what you think might be important will rarely bring success. You'd have to be incredibly lucky for your work history, and the extracts you have included, to match an organization's primary needs at that time.

Sure, some few lucky applicants out of hundreds have resumes that are the closest to the company's needs at a certain time and are invited to interview. Your chances depend a lot on the number of applicants for a specific job. I've known of really great jobs for which there were hundreds, even a thousand applicants. Prospective employers usually like to see three to five "finalists" face-to-face. Even if there are only a hundred good applicants you have only a five percent chance of getting invited to an interview.

● WHY NOT SEND YOUR PROSPECTIVE EMPLOYER A RESUME THAT COVERS EVERYTHING?

You could write a life history that would cover ninety percent of everything you've done or can remember without prompting by knowing the hiring company's real needs. But it would go on and on for many pages. Unless you have an incredibly interesting background and are already a celebrity, who would read it? If you can get someone to do that, you'd probably do better to write your autobiography as a book and forget about a job. However, even if you could get prospective employers to read an autobiography with everything in it, it will contain some work experiences that would cause an organization to automatically reject you. That leads to the second reason you need to avoid using a resume. Professionals call these experiences unwanted by an employer "knockout factors."

● ALL RESUMES CONTAIN KNOCKOUT FACTORS

"Knockout factors" are experiences in your background not desired by your prospective employer that will "knock you out" from getting the interview. All headhunters know about them. In fact, headhunters usually ask their clients for them when they get the job order and before they begin to recruit for a position. That way, they'll know who must not be submitted as candidates.

There are several aspects about knockout factors that you should find interesting. First, knockout factors vary from job to job. In fact, what might be a knockout factor in one company, another company might find highly desirable. For example, one company had a bias against hiring salespeople from a particular geographical area. However, at the same time, another company wanted to hire salespeople *only* from that geographical area!

Usually a knockout factor will not affect your ability to perform well in that company, even though the company may think this is true. One company I know did not want to hire former military officers. They thought that hard-driving former military managers would clash with their laid-back style of doing business. However, one day a former officer got hired because he was a relative of the president. He turned out to be the best division manager this company ever hired and was soon a vice president due to his own abilities.

Finally, and most important for our purposes, if you can somehow get the interview, even though you have a knockout factor, you can still get the job anyway. Every headhunter can tell you a story something like the one I'm going to tell you from his or her own professional experience.

Interviews Overcome Knockout Factors

About twenty-five years ago, I was a young headhunter and my client asked me to recruit a drilling engineer in the petroleum industry. I took down all the details of the job order so I knew exactly what they wanted. I asked about knockout factors and was told that it was essential that any candidate I submitted not have a lot of experience in the oil fields of California. "Why not?" I asked. "For this particular job, we feel that California experience ruins drilling engineers for what we want them to do," I was told. "What if I find an unusually outstanding drilling engineer who has a lot of experience in California?" I asked. "Would you be willing to take a look at him?" "Under no circumstances," my client answered. "If the candidate has more than a few months in California, we don't want to hear about him."

I left my client and began a telephone journey around the country. I made more than a hundred telephone calls. I talked to dozens of petroleum engineers and followed numerous leads, many of them false, looking for candidates. I needed three to five petroleum engineers who met all of the requirements of the job order, were employed and happy in their jobs, were willing to move for a better opportunity and met the knock-out factor requirement of not having a lot of drilling experience in California.

Why three to five candidates? First, most clients want to see more than one candidate. Moreover, human beings being human beings, in some cases the client will not like the candidate; in other cases, the candidate won't like the client. In some cases neither will like each other. The expectation is that with multiple candidates, at least one will like the client and visa versa.

Of course, we were well compensated for accomplishing this task successfully. If a client hired one of our candidates, we received about one third of his annual salary as a fee. This came from the company, and was not from a deduction from the new hire's annual wages. If one of our candidates wasn't hired, we got nothing. So, we were well motivated to pay attention to detail, work hard, and do a good job.

This search took me about two weeks. I had been in touch with the client on a regular basis so the client wasn't too surprised when I called by telephone to verbally present the five candidates I'd unearthed so they could be flown out for interviews. I knew I had a winner in that group!

Not so fast, Cohen. When I called, my client sounded hesitant. "Oh, look Bill, I hate to tell you this, but we just filled the position about an hour ago." I mentally saw my fee flap its wings and disappear into the distance.

"Wonderful," I managed to say, assisted by pushing the mean end of a pencil into my left palm—a stunt accomplished despite the fact that I was holding the telephone in that hand. I tried to take the high road despite having just learned I had worked for no compensation for the past two weeks. "I'm sure you're very relieved to have finally hired someone," I cooed.

After a mumbled agreement, I asked if my would-be client if he would spend a few minutes going over his new hire's background. "It will help me to recruit for you in the future," I explained. This was standard procedure when we lost one, because if we understood the kind of candidate the client was likely to hire, it helped us in our future recruiting for him.

We went over his new petroleum engineer's work experience. You guessed it. Most of their new engineer's experience was from the oil fields of California. "Wasn't that a knock-out factor?" I asked innocently.

"Oh, yeah," he mumbled. "I guess that's true. But you know, he just happened to call in here and we didn't ask where he had worked. It never came up. We saw him face-to-face and he was such a great guy, with a terrific background in the oil business, I don't think its going to make any difference."

As I said, every headhunter can tell you this kind of story, because once a candidate gets to the face-to-face interview stage, all bets are off. Interviewees can get hired regardless of what they have or have not done, or what is in their background. But, any resume can have knockout factors, so if you use a resume, it's like playing Russian Roulette as to what knockout factors you have for a particular job.

● SHOULD YOU EVER USE A RESUME?

There are just two times when you should use a resume. One is if you can't get an interview without one. This usually happens in a large organization and begins when you are contacted by human resources (HR), the employment office, or the personnel department—whatever they chose to call these folks in this particular company. They can't imagine someone getting a job without a resume. You have gone right to your potential boss as I explained in the previous chapter. But in his company, either he had to send the request to interview you through HR, and that's why a representative of HR is calling, or someone passed your sales letter, fax, or e-mail to HR.

First, you should try to avoid sending a resume. Say, that you've done so much that it would take a book to record it all, so you don't have one. If you are told that you can't get an interview without a resume, ask if you can bring the resume with you to the interview. Remember, you can be hired from an interview no matter what you've done previously. If you are still told you must send a resume first, say, "Okay, but I need to know everything I can about the job . . . otherwise we're talking fifty pages and it will take me a week to put one together." Then, find out all you can. You'd be surprised what a difference that can make in the resume you send. Until you have your interview, you still won't know all you can, but you will be 1,000% better off than sending a "one size fits all resume."

The second time you should send a resume is after the interview if you don't get a job offer. If you receive a job offer, don't send one. If you follow this advice, what will probably happen then is that someone in HR will contact you several weeks after you start work. They will apologize for losing your resume and will ask if you have another copy you can send to them. I know, this has actually happened to me. You can then put something together to send to satisfy their great need to keep this paperwork on file.

If you didn't get an offer after the interview, put together a special resume. Naturally it will emphasize your accomplishments in the light of what is important to that company. Because you got this information during the interview (I'll show you how to do this is a later chapter) you should have no difficulty avoiding knockout factors, which you may have also picked up on during the interview. If you had to put something together to get the interview, call this an "updated resume" and make sure they throw the old one out.

Now if you aren't going to use a resume to get an interview, what are you going to use? We'll see in Chapter 7.

● WHY YOU NEED A RESUME

Even though you aren't going to distribute a generic resume to everyone and his brother, you do need to develop a good one right from the start. Why? A job campaign is a sales campaign. A good sales person knows his or her product inside and out. The truth is, no matter how well you think you know yourself, you have forgotten a great deal that you have accomplished which will be of great interest to prospective employers. Moreover, you have to take your experiences, and translate them into accomplishments. You will need the contents of a comprehensive resume as a basis for the very powerful methods of getting interviews I will show you in later chapters.

● TAKE THE TIME TO DO IT RIGHT

If you get your resume right at this stage, you will save considerable time later. So before you are tempted to dust off an old resume and add a couple of lines, read the rest of this chapter.

● WHY YOU SHOULDN'T GO TO A RESUME WRITER

Some job hunters recognize that the resume is important to their campaign, but they do not want to take the time to develop the resume they need. They do a very natural thing. They turn to a professional resume writer. Don't make that mistake. It is essential to your campaign that you prepare your own resume.

To begin with, no one knows you as you know yourself. Even if the professional resume writer spends several hours with you (and most will not), consider how long you have spent with yourself. You cannot remember everything you should during the time you interview with a professional resume writer or complete a questionnaire, no matter how comprehensive. Important facts will occur to you later, as your campaign proceeds. Even more important, small items that you considered incidental to your career will assume a more primary role for a particular job. The professional resume writer, not knowing you as you know yourself and not being a part of your campaign, will fix in concrete at the beginning a resume based on only what he knows about you at that time. No matter how well written, this resume may be useless only days into your campaign.

Every professional resume writer has a particular style—good, bad, or indifferent. You may like the style or not. The point is, it is not your style. Many people who receive large numbers of resumes have learned to spot the styles of certain professional resume-writing firms. Inevitably the thought must occur to them that a resume prepared for you, and not by you, indicates a lack of writing ability or a lack of self-confidence in written communication.

In developing your own resume and wording your experiences and accomplishments properly, you will have a chance to think about your career in a logical fashion. You cannot do this if you fill out a form or discuss your background with someone. You cannot do it by reading over what someone else has interpreted your career to be. You must take the time to organize these facts yourself. This is not easy, but it will be worth the effort. The experience will help you later in writing a sales letter, electronic or otherwise, answering advertisements, and discussing your background on the telephone or in face-to-face interviews.

A professional resume-writing service, whatever it costs, is a misallocation of your financial resources. Remember, any job campaign costs money. Unless you are financially independent and don't need to work, it is important to allocate your financial resources where they do the most good. Hiring someone else to write your resume will waste money that you could spend more profitably elsewhere.

● HOW TO DEVELOP YOUR OWN RESUME

The type of resume that I will show you how to write is not one that many employment counselors would encourage. There is good reason for this. Much of the information commonly put in resumes and subsequently distributed to prospective employers has little bearing not only on whether you will be hired, but even on whether you will be invited in for an interview. You cannot attain the first without the second. The sole purpose of sending information to a PE, whether through a resume or an extract, is to obtain an interview. No one will hire you on the basis of a resume alone; you will be hired only on the basis of a face-to-face interview. Therefore, your resume and subsequent sales letters, answers to advertisements, and telephone conversations must be geared to achieving that objective: the interview. That is the kind of resume I want you to prepare.

Begin with the information you wrote down about your next job from Chapter 3. The reason for starting off with this information is to help you to keep your job objective constantly in mind as you develop your resume. You cannot skip this step and finish with a superior resume, just as you cannot perform calculus without first having prepared yourself with algebra.

Take your time in preparing your resume. It should take you several hours to complete even a sketchy outline. Use the following outline to ensure that your resume is as complete as possible:

My Next Job Position

Title

Function and Level of Responsibility

Specific Responsibilities

Who Position Will Report To

Salary Range

Industry

Type of Company

Geographical Location

Career History

Dates of Employment

Company Name

Annual Sales Volume

Type of Product or Service

Titles and Positions Held

Supervisor

Starting and Ending Salary

Reason for Leaving

Job Responsibilities

For each position, include budget, number of people supervised and titles of those supervised, responsibilities for money, equipment, and material and any other quantification of your responsibilities you can think of.

Accomplishments

This is very important. Experience and accomplishments are not the same. Be specific and quantify all accomplishments. Relate them to sales, profits, and cost savings, whenever possible. List at least five accomplishments for every position you held in every company. You can express them as dollars, percentages, or actual numbers. For example, "Responsible for personnel interviews" is experience. "Conducted 343 personnel interviews," is an accomplishment.

The following examples show the difference between experiences and accomplishments.

- *Experience:* "General Manager of a chain of 7 health food stores. Supervised 47 employees doing $3,000,000 in annual sales."
- *Accomplishment:* "Built health food store chain from 0 to 7 stores in 18 months. Broke even after first 4 months with total profitability of $298,000."
- *Experience:* "Software designer for 3 years."
- *Accomplishment:* "Designed 13 major programs. One designed as an easy accounting system for doctors and dentists was the first successful program for this purpose. It became a best seller with 21,000 units sold at $900 to $1,200 each."
- *Experience:* "Computer lab assistant for 3 years."
- *Accomplishment:* "Counseled 376 students, and 7 professors. This saved 1,532 man-hours."
- *Experience:* "Consultant; I developed and presented a marketing plan for a start-up business."
- *Accomplishment:* "The marketing plan I developed will result in first year sales of $275,000 and breakeven in 3 months."

- *Experience:* "Part-time salesman at Topline Furniture Store."
- *Accomplishment:* "Made 76 sales presentations and sold $18,760 in product. Given recognition 3 times as top salesman of the quarter."

Articulating your accomplishments may not be easy. No organization keeps track of what you do quantitatively and you probably have not done so either. So you need to think deeply about what you actually accomplished in every position you held, what good things happened as a result of your actions, and if possible associate this with a number or sales figure. By the way, note that all figures are stated with numbers and not written out. That's the way you want to use this information later as well. That way, the numbers stand out.

Here's how I helped one gentleman who held the not particularly impressive job of shoe salesman for eighteen months. Our conversation went something like this:

"I was a shoe salesman for 18 months."

"How many shoes did you sell altogether?"

"I don't know."

"How many days did you work in a week?"

"Six days."

"How many weeks did you work a year?"

"Well, I had two weeks vacation. We also got a couple days off for Christmas and a few days off for other holidays. I guess on the average I'd say about 48 weeks."

"So, over the year and a half you worked a total of six days times 48 plus 24 weeks, or 432 days. Is that right?"

"I guess so."

"Tell me, on average, how many pairs of shoes did you sell in a day?"

"Oh, I don't know . . . maybe six to ten."

"Can we say eight?"

"Yeah, I guess so."

"How much did these shoes sell for?"

"About $50 on the low side, right on up to $200."

"Could you give me an overall average?"

"$100 is probably pretty close."

"So you sold eight shoes at about $100 each for 432 days."

(After consulting a calculator).

"Did you know you had sold $345,600 worth of shoes?"

"Wow, really!?"

"Yes, that's one accomplishment."

This demonstrates a technique you can work on yourself. One other note: don't round figures off and use words like "approximately" or "about." Accomplishments developed this way are estimates. Since you are estimating anyway, it's better to estimate an uneven figure rather than a rounded-off one, because it's more believable.

Successful Management Recommendations

List recommendations you made on organization, administration, or management that were partially or fully implemented, and their results. Again, quantify whenever you can.

Successful Technical Recommendations

List recommendations you made on technical aspects of your job that were fully or partially implemented and their results. Quantify them wherever you can.

Promotions and Transfers

List all promotions and transfers of assignment while with the company, along with salary increases and increases in responsibilities.

Awards, Honors, and Commendations

List every honor, award, or commendation received in every job in every company. Include verbal recommendations if significant.

Reports, Documents, and Published Articles

Describe reports, documents, and published articles you wrote and those that were prepared under your direction. Describe any special significance attached to any.

Concurrent Away-from-Job Experience/Accomplishments

Describe your "extracurricular" activities during this period. Include social activities, church, club, association, etc. Include offices held and quantified accomplishments.

Special Qualifications

List special qualifications requiring licenses or special training and experience. This would include foreign languages.

Associations

List professional associations, offices held, and quantified accomplishments.

Special Accomplishments

List articles, books, copyrights, inventions, and similar accomplishments.

Current Recreational Interests

List hobbies, athletics, and other interests. Make special note of accomplishments—for example, "grand master chess champion."

Professional Training

List courses, dates, and schools; programs, and special courses.

Education

List schools, dates, degrees, majors, and special scholastic honors.

Review each heading. Don't leave anything out. This will ensure that important information needed for your campaign is recalled, documented, and kept together in an organized fashion for immediate use. It will focus your thinking on experiences and accomplishments, both in your career and outside of work that supports your job position objectives. It will increase your self-confidence immeasurably, as you see before you the unique experiences and accomplishments that you alone can offer to a PE. Finally, it will save you a considerable amount of time during your campaign.

● THE IMPORTANCE OF SPECIAL ASSIGNMENTS

Information on special and short assignments in your career and special experience outside of your regular work is frequently overlooked, but it can be vital to your campaign.

Tim 0. spent years working as a human factors engineer with a large aerospace company but was faced with a certain layoff. The three months he spent working on ejection seat requirements got him a job as project engineer in charge of the development of a new ejection seat. Special, short, and outside-of-work assignments can be the deciding factor in getting you an interview and getting you a job. Often, the same has been true of my students who have followed my methods. Some have obtained incredible jobs, at high levels, although they may have never worked previously.

One of my graduate students, Luis E. was a foreign national. Luis obtained a job with a major consulting firm. Yet, he had never worked previously, and he did not graduate from a "name" university. He relied entirely on his experience as a student . . . that was all he had! He used his classroom accomplishments and his accomplishments during extracurricular activities around campus.

Luis did not talk about his "A" grades or his grade point average. These are accomplishments, but research shows that they are usually not very useful in obtaining a great job. The accomplishments I am talking about are the results or potential results of marketing plans he developed, marketing research he did, teams that he led, and the results of his holding office in a campus club. He got the highest salary ever from his university.

Your resume will change considerably as your campaign progresses. You will think of new items to add, other accomplishments to emphasize, and other aspects of your career which you decide to de-emphasize. You will find this happening right up to the last day of your campaign.

The Main Point

Avoid sending a resume to a prospective employer unless he or she refuses to see you without one. Never send out generic resumes under any circumstances. Still, take the time to prepare a comprehensive resume based on your accomplishments, quantified whenever possible.

EMPHASIZE YOUR EXPERIENCE

6

How to Emphasize Your Accomplishments

"I sent out 351 sales letters emphasizing my accomplishments as you suggested and received five interviews. Then I followed up by telephoning 87 of these who had not responded and got an additional 12 interviews. And what interviews! They flew me all over the country, and I really felt greatly in demand. After 12 weeks, I'd had enough and I accepted a great offer."

— General Manager

The secret that will get you as many interviews as you want is to write and employ powerful personal sales letters, without a resume, which emphasize not your experience, but your accomplishments. Done right, these will consistently get interviews which lead to job offers. You can use conventional snail mail, fax, or e-mail. All three methods work well.

Sales letters are the best, and next to telephone calls, the fastest method of generating interviews that lead to job offers for great jobs. Job hunters have proven this over and over on the firing line. For this reason, I urge you to emphasize this method above all others in your campaign. A personal sales letter is one or two pages long and addressed right to your prospective employer (PE) by name and title. It describes your outstanding accomplishments by quantifying them in such a way that the PE is convinced you are an exceptional candidate for the job.

I promise you that the results of mailing personal sales letters will amaze you; you will be invited in for interviews regardless of the present state of the economy and regardless of your past lack of success in generating interviews. And if you use this technique and the copywriter's formula that I'll give you in the next chapter, you're going to get interviews faster than you ever imagined.

In this chapter, I'll introduce the concept of the sales letter and explain why they work. I'll show you how to package and use them and explain what results you can expect. In the next chapter, I'll show you exactly how to write them.

● AN INSTANT FLY-OUT TWO DAYS AFTER OPENING A CAMPAIGN

Only a few weeks before I wrote these lines, one of my graduate students decided to open his campaign by using this wonderful method along with my formula to respond to eight job openings he discovered on the internet. He disregarded the instructions to send resumes to the respective human resources departments. Instead, he sent a personal sales letter by e-mail using my formula directly to each of his eight prospective bosses. Within two days he had a phone call from one of them who immediately made reservations at the company's expense to fly him out for a personal interview. Personal sales letters done right work fast!

● THE ADVANTAGES OF USING PERSONAL LETTERS TO GET INTERVIEWS

There are several advantages in using sales letters for getting interviews. The quality of interview derived from a personal sales letter is higher than that derived from any other source. This means a higher offer-to-interview ratio and less wasted time.

Personal sales letters also generate more predictable results than other methods of gaining interviews. You will be able to predict roughly how many interviews you will receive for each batch of sales letters you send out. I will discuss this in more detail later.

When you send out personal sales letters, you frequently will have little competition for interviews and little or no competition for a job offer. If you respond to an advertisement in *The Wall Street Journal* or a large city newspaper, you may be competing with 500, sometimes 1,000 or more job hunters for the same position. When you send a personal sales letter, the position may not even be advertised, the company's personnel or human resources department may not have been notified, and you may be the only candidate for the job. Imagine presenting your superior qualifications to the hiring executive under these circumstances!

In a personal sales letter you can tailor your experience and accomplishments to the exact specifications (function, level, type of company) of the job you are seeking. When you tailor your response to an advertisement, you are trying to fit someone else's requirements. In the personal sales letter, you write to fill *your* requirements.

● SALES LETTERS AVOID "KNOCKOUT FACTORS"

Using sales letters instead of sending resumes also lets you avoid the problem of knockout factors. This is because sales letters concentrate on presenting your accomplishments in a brief and forceful manner against a single job objective. Its brevity greatly reduces the chances for some factor—one you may even consider favorable—to eliminate you prior to the interview.

● ARE PERSONAL SALES LETTERS REALLY THAT EFFECTIVE?

You bet they are! Jim B. had no experience in job hunting. He had been with the same company for 14 years when he suddenly found himself out of a job. Jim mailed out 1,000 sales letters. Within six weeks he had five firm job offers, all of them at a considerable increase in salary. Even though Jim was out of work, and even though he had not been a supervisor under his former employer, he sought a job only at the supervisory level. All the job offers he received were in this category. Jim accepted the best of the offers. For a month afterward he had to turn down requests for additional interviews. Was his personal sales letter effective? What do you think?

● WHY PERSONAL SALES LETTERS ARE SO POWERFUL

Obviously, your PE is not sitting and waiting for your personal sales letter to arrive. Why, then, is this technique so powerful? At any given time a certain percentage of executives with hiring authority will have personnel needs that must be fulfilled. They may have just begun to think about the problem or may even have extended someone an offer and be awaiting acceptance.

Maybe a president is thinking about replacing a vice president or creating a new position at a high level; or it could be a sales manager recognizing the need for additional salespeople. At another company, an operations officer's production manager has just given him two weeks notice. Personnel problems can appear suddenly even at the top levels when a chairman of the board recognizes that a president needs to retire immediately because of poor health.

So the recipients of your personal sales letter have their own problems. It is the exact opposite of yours and they may or may not have begun to work on finding the man or woman they need. On any given day, in some organization, a certain percentage of PEs will need someone with the skills and experience you possess. The success of your personal sales letter stems from the fact that the product you describe (yourself) by your accomplishments fills a definite need at this particular time.

Of course, the higher the level of position you are seeking, the fewer positions will be open to you. A company may need many engineers but only one vice president of engineering. However, if you contact enough PEs, some will have openings at your level, whatever it is. In many cases you will have very little or no competition at all, since your PE may not yet have started a search.

YOUR OBJECTIVE IN WRITING A PERSONAL SALES LETTER

Whatever level of responsibility you are seeking, your task is to construct a personal sales letter that generates the greatest number of responses from PEs, whether or not they have started to actively look for someone. If your letter tries to attract attention by emphasizing what you want, rather than what your PE needs, it will in all probability end up in the wastepaper basket. So don't talk about your goals and objectives, no matter how important you think they are.

Your letter should clearly show your reader how you can solve his or her problem, not just by filling a position but by helping to maximize profits, raise efficiency, lower overhead, increase sales, save on taxes, or whatever else your talents can achieve. If it does, your PE will practically demand to see you for an interview. Wouldn't you, in his or her place?

As you write your personal sales letter, keep in mind that your immediate objective is to get a face-to-face interview. Many job hunters put everything possible in their personal sales letter in the belief that their immediate purpose is to get hired. This is a mistake. As I explained before, for most jobs you cannot get hired without a face-to-face interview. Your personal sales letter will help you achieve that vital objective. So, in your letter you must show your PE that what you want is closely connected with what he wants, and is in his own best interests; that by doing what you suggest he is furthering his own ends. In short, your sales letter must show that your qualifications are the solution to the PE's problem.

YOUR OWN AND YOUR PE'S NEEDS—HOW TO SATISFY BOTH

Your needs will be satisfied when you have obtained the great job that you desire. The PE's needs will be satisfied when he or she hires a superior executive or professional to fill the open position. You have already taken a giant step toward bringing these two needs together by establishing a precise professional objective and researching and developing an outstanding resume, even though you are not going to send it to anyone as a generic promotional tool. In the personal sales letter you are the product; and if you have taken the necessary time to analyze your needs, accomplishments, experiences, and capabilities, you should now know your product very well indeed.

Let's look again at your PE's needs and requirements. If you were a sales manager in a company selling a sophisticated product—say, electronic data processing (EDP) equipment, what kind of salespeople would you want to hire? What kind of background would you look for? Write down your own ideal job specifications for this position. Mine include a track record of success in selling technical products, experience in the EDP industry, and a technical degree.

How about a senior buyer who supervises three other buyers in a medium-size company in the electronics industry? You would probably look for past accomplishment as a buyer in the electronics industry and past success as a supervisor, or as the number-two person in a department of buyers.

Let's try a personnel manager in the insurance industry supervising two other personnel specialists. You would look for someone with a record of success as a personnel manager, successful supervisory experience in the personnel career field, experience in the insurance industry, and a business degree, preferably specializing in personnel.

Notice that the key words in all these examples relate to prior successful experience in the same or a similar function. But what if you don't have industry experience? Are you still a viable candidate?

● HOW TO SATISFY A PROSPECTIVE EMPLOYER'S NEEDS EVEN IF YOU DON'T HAVE INDUSTRY EXPERIENCE

Again, even if you are a new graduate, classroom experience relative to the job can be of equal value. That you have the experience to do the job is what is important, no matter where you obtained it.

If every one of his or her requirements cannot be met, the PE will usually be willing to compromise, provided the primary specifications of the job are met by outstanding accomplishments. Few would fail to hire a technical salesman who has proven himself by an outstanding record in technical sales, even if he had no degree.

In constructing your personal sales letter, you should strive to meet every possible requirement that a PE would seek. Keep your PE's needs in mind as you develop your sales letter, and present your qualifications so that these needs are filled. This doesn't mean lying or in any way misrepresenting yourself. It does mean emphasizing what you have to offer that is relevant to the job.

● WHAT YOU SHOULD NOT SAY IN YOUR SALES LETTER

As I mentioned previously, and as I will emphasize throughout this book, it is to your advantage not to send a resume to a PE until after the interview. Therefore, do not mention a resume in any context in your sales letter. If you do, at best you will be asked to send it. Then, if your resume is received favorably (and at this point the odds are against it) you will be invited in for an interview. This is not what you are after. You want an immediate interview. You will not attain this objective if you mention a resume.

Never ruin the specialized image you have carefully built in the explanation of your letter by indicating that you are ready to consider some other type of job. If you do, your PE may feel you are so much in need of a job you will consider anything. PEs like to deal with winners, not desperate job hunters. If the PE volunteers a different type of job and asks about your interest, you can consider that opportunity on its own merits. But it's up to the PE to initiate such a discussion. You must not even hint of the possibility in your sales letter.

Finally, if you are currently unemployed you should recognize that knowledge of your unemployment can devalue your worth with a PE if it is disclosed too early in your campaign. I will show you how to deal with being unemployed later in the book. Actually, there are definite advantages to being unemployed in job hunting. However, you should not reveal your unemployment in your sales letter.

HOW TO DEVELOP MAILING OR E-MAIL LISTS OF PEs

There are many excellent directories you can use to prepare your mailing list of PEs. But, a few words of caution are in order. Make certain the directory is current; an out-of-date directory is a waste of time and resources and will cut down on the percentage of responses. Use only those directories that provide names as well as companies. You will direct your sales letters not to titles, but to names and titles.

There are directories listing executives in every conceivable industry. Check your library first to see what directories are available. If you can find them, consult the *Guide to American Directories for Compiling Mailing Lists* and *Principal Business Directories for Building Mailing Lists*. Both volumes list more than 1,000 different directories that can be used as sources for PEs in various industries. The following directories are general in content, the numbers listed change frequently, and they offer an approximation only. Most are going on-line if they are not already.

Dun & Bradstreet's Million Dollar Directory has moved on-line. D&B Million Dollar Database provides the information professional, marketer and sales executive with information on over 1.3 million leading U.S. public and private businesses. Company information includes industry information with up to 24 individual 8-digit SICs, size criteria (employees and annual sales), type of ownership, and a list of principal executives with biographies.

Hoover's Handbook of American Business is a two-volume set that contains in-depth profiles of 750 of America's largest and most influential companies. Also on CD Rom is *Hoover's Company Capsules* with information on 11,000 major U.S. companies, which includes 30,000 executive names.

The *Standard & Poor's Register of Corporations, Directors and Executives* is a set of three volumes published annually. Three supplements are issued throughout the year, in April, July, and October, providing details of changes which have occurred since publication of the annual volumes.

Standard Directory of Advertisers lists 80,000 executives of 17,000 companies advertising nationally.

Thomas Register of American Manufacturers includes 100,000-plus manufacturers by product and location. They are on-line at http://www.thomasregister .com.

Of course, there are plenty of other directories available on the internet. Plus, you can locate company officers through their web pages. Here are a few internet directories to start with:

http://www.BigBook.com

http://www.fortune.com/fortune/fortune500/The Fortune 500

http://www.imarketinc.com/

http://dowjones.wsj.com

One site, http://www.donnelleymarketing.com/, allows you to order lists on-line. You can order lists of executives in certain industries, geographical areas, functional areas, and so on.

Finally, check out the Kelsey Group at http://www.kelseygroup.com for their listing of URLs for yellow page directories, white page directories, business directories, and more.

● WHY YOU SHOULD MAIL YOUR OWN SALES LETTERS

Some firms will offer to mail your sales letter (or resume) to hundreds or thousands of companies at a cost that seems extremely reasonable. For example, one firm advertised that it will put your letters in the hands of 5,000 companies for less than $500. Since the postage alone would cost you much more than this amount, it seems like a good buy. Why isn't it? To begin with, these firms can only make money by mailing your sales letter along with those of many other job seekers at the same time. Usually, this packet of information is sent not to the hiring executive, but to the human resources department. This is not where you want a description of your accomplishments to go. Moreover, even if it went to the hiring executive, it would arrive in a packet with the letters or resumes of other competitors. It would not go in the highly personalized fashion that is essential for a successful sales letter campaign.

That's not all. Since you did not develop the mailing list, you have no idea where your letter is being sent (size of company, geographical area, and so forth). It could even go to your own firm. And since you have no idea who was on the original mailing list, there is no way you can send a second letter to those executives who did not invite you in for an interview. And sometimes this is not a bad tactic since need for people, even high level people, sometimes changes very frequently.

Finally, this method of scattering your accomplishments tends to lower your overall value, especially if, as sometimes happens, an executive receives more than one copy of your letter in the same mail. For all these reasons, I urge you to handle your own mailing.

HOW TO COMPILE A LIST OF EXECUTIVE RECRUITERS

You can also send a personal letter to executive recruiters using this technique, and the formula I'll give you.

Here are some sources for names of executive recruiters. Again, the numbers are approximations only:

Consultants and Consulting Organizations Directory, by Virgil L. Burton, III (editor), is published by the Gale Group. It contains information on 5,000 consulting firms, including approximately 500 executive recruiters. This guide is very expensive. Check with a library first.

Directory of Executive Recruiters 2000, published by Kennedy Publications, Lists 2,300 search firms throughout the United States.

The Global 200 Executive Recruiters: An Essential Guide to the Best Recruiters in the United States, Europe, Asia, and Latin America, by Nancy Garrison Jenn, is published by Jossey Bass.

Executive Recruiters Almanac, edited by Steven Graber, is published by Adams Media Corporation. It lists recruiters by state and specialty.

List of Members, published by the Association of Executive Recruiting Consultants, Inc., 30 Rockefeller Plaza, New York, New York 10020, lists approximately 60 member firms.

The Executive Employment Guide is published by the American Management Associations, 135 West 50th Street, New York, New York 10020. Updated frequently, it contains information on 129 executive recruiting firms.

Directories such as these frequently go out of print and are discontinued. Also, many are expensive. I don't recommend purchasing those that are costly. Instead, go to your library. Your librarian can help you find the latest directories that are available, and it won't cost you a penny.

One of the best sources for names of executive recruiters is your telephone book. Also, go to your library for phone books covering other cities and states. Don't limit yourself geographically in mailing your sales letters. Even if an executive recruiter works only for a local firm, he will usually recruit candidates from all over the country.

Address your sales letter to Director, XYZ and Associates. If you know a specific recruiter at a firm, use the individual's name. However, the search industry has such a tremendous turnover that, unlike the sources of companies for your sales letters, any directory of recruiters' names will be obsolete after six months. No matter what source you use, your list of executive recruiters is likely to be only 50 percent accurate.

HOW TO PACKAGE YOUR SALES LETTERS

There is an old saying that you can't tell a book by its cover. That may be true, but it is irrelevant. The first judgment people make about a book is by its cover, whether the contents are any good or not.

The same is true about you and your personal sales letter. For this reason, you should take great care in printing your sales letter. It may be the only representation of you that the PE or the executive recruiter has until the interview. The letter and envelope should be of high-quality paper, with at least 25 percent rag content. The printing—your address on the letterhead and your name and address on the envelope—should be of equally high quality. I recommend a process called thermographing, which gives the appearance of engraved print.

I most definitely recommend monarch-size stationery ($7\frac{1}{4}'' \times 10\frac{1}{2}''$). I like the monarch size because many senior executives use it. It will give your letter a very classy image. Your letter will also have a better chance of getting through the executive's secretary and directly into the hands of the hiring executive because it will look less like a resume. Resumes are almost always standard size. The only disadvantage of monarch-size stationery is that you may need to use two sheets, which will increase your costs. To locate monarch size stationery, call a stationery supply store. Most printers don't carry it.

Through the magic of a computer and a merge program, every letter can have the appearance of being individually typed. All you do is type up the basic list of addresses and your letter separately. Follow the merge instructions of your word processing program and in a few minutes, you will accomplish what once took hours. If you don't have a computer, and can't borrow the use of one, you will have to pay for these services. They are essential. A typed letter, which was once fully acceptable, is much less so today. Computers have made everything look more professional and spoiled us all.

On no account should you use the sales letter as a cover sheet for your resume. If you do, forget the whole thing. You will not get the results I described. You must send the personal sales letter by itself.

THE RESULTS YOU CAN EXPECT FROM SALES LETTERS

Some highly marketable individuals who select their target companies extremely well and do everything else right have reported letter-to-interview returns of as high as 50 percent. But such results are rare. Anything in the 2- to 5-percent range is normal. If you hit 10 percent, you are doing incredibly well. If you get a three percent response, you will get 30 interviews on a mailing of 1,000 sales letters. This, along with other methods of generating interviews described in this book, is probably more than adequate for you to obtain a great job. If your rate is less than 2 percent, you should consider revising your sales letter. Sometimes a minor change or omission of one statement will raise your returns several percentage points. Reread your sales letter several times to see if you can spot what might be turning your PEs off.

Remember, I am talking about actual interviews generated as a result of your sales letters. Replies in themselves count for nothing. If all 1,000 PEs respond to your letters, but do not invite you in for an interview, your results are 0 percent. But if you are on target with your material, you can expect 30 to 50 interviews per 1,000 sales letters.

My student, Mike G. at the University of Southern California, was desperate for a job. He was unsuccessful in getting even a single interview through the university's Career Development Center. When he came to see me, it was less than a month before graduation, marriage, and no job. Following my instructions, he wrote a sales letter in accordance with the formula in the next chapter. He sent his letters out as soon as his fiancée typed them up. Before graduation, he had several offers and accepted the best one. He told me that he had so many calls for interviews, he had to start turning them down! What with finals and the interviews he had scheduled, he didn't have the time. Amazingly, Mike sent out only 39 sales letters. That's a record that still stands.

THE TYPES OF RESPONSES YOU WILL RECEIVE

Most of the responses you receive from your sales letters will be rejects. Some will come directly from the hiring executive. Others will originate from the personnel/human resources/employment department, in which case you may well get a form letter. Such a reply will read along these lines: "Mr. Smith, whom you have written, has asked that I respond. Though your qualifications are superior, your resume has been circulated throughout the company and there are no openings for someone of your background at the present time. However, because conditions may change, I have taken the liberty of placing your resume in our current file and will contact you should any openings arise. Thanks again for considering the XYZ Company."

If you get such a notice, it may surprise you to learn that Mr. Smith probably has not seen your letter. And it is doubtful that your "resume" was circulated throughout the company, especially since, if you followed my instructions, you never sent one. Your qualifications were probably matched against a list of current requirements on file in the human resources department. That took about fifteen seconds, and then they sent you a form letter, not even bothering to notice that you sent a letter, and not a resume.

I once received a rejection notice from a company that had already extended me a job offer. How is that possible? I wrote two different officers at the company, both of whom might have needed someone with my qualifications. During my interview I learned that the other executive I had written was out of town. This executive's secretary had intercepted the letter and forwarded it to the employment department. So routine was this action, and the written response, that the personnel manager didn't recognize my name, or recall that I had an offer pending with the company.

Another, more insidious type of rejection from the human resources department is the employment application. You will be sent a form to complete "so that the PE can better assess your opportunities with the firm." I recommend that you not waste time filling out an employment form unless you are certain that a specific job is available. Otherwise, you risk giving out important information about yourself for no gain at all. For example, even if you don't give your references, it is unwise to list your previous employers at this early stage. The PE may call these companies even if you have no interest in the job. (Maybe they are not hiring anyone right now, and the personnel person hasn't anything better to do.) Premature and needless reference checks can hurt you. If repeated, it can irritate those people who are asked to comment on your past performance, even if they like you. I mean, the first couple of times they give you the enthusiastic boost you deserve. However, what about the ninth or tenth time they're called? Are they still as enthusiastic? This will also break your security if you are conducting a campaign in secret.

What are your possible courses of action? You can treat the employment form as a rejection and write a second sales letter to the PE, following the standard procedure with all rejections. I'll show you how to do that shortly. You can contact the individual who sent you the employment application and try to determine if a specific job opening exists.

Or you can fill out the employment application without giving references, names of former supervisors, names of former companies, *or* other information that could compromise your position. I'll tell you how you must handle requests for references in Chapter 13. For employers, use general descriptions: "a large insurance company," "a major aerospace company," "a well-known consulting firm." For references, use a general title, without the name, address, or phone number: "vice president of a medium-size company," "state senator." Enclose a note stating that complete information will be furnished if there is mutual interest. I like that. It tells the recipient that you are not an applicant. You aren't applying for anything. You are a potential candidate . . . if you become interested.

Some letters will request additional information or a resume. Try to obtain more information by telephone; then decide whether to comply with the request.

● HOW TO HANDLE REQUESTS FOR INTERVIEWS

Some invitations for interviews are worded so weakly that you may have difficulty recognizing them. Usually they are sent when a PE is afraid of building up your hopes for a job. Such a letter of invitation might read like this: "Though we have no immediate needs, I would like to talk with you if you have the time. Please call ahead for this appointment. Sorry we don't have anything." These requests, no matter how weak, should be followed up.

It has been my experience that most requests for interviews come by telephone rather than by mail. This is one reason that it is important for your telephone number to be readily located in your sales letter. Several books I have read on job hunting urge the job hunter to avoid being interviewed over the telephone at all costs. One even suggests that you hang up rather than respond. You will soon discover, however, that with the popularity of making appointments by phone, most PEs will do some interviewing this way. If the PE is going to pay your travel expenses for the interview, you can bet that he will want to know more than you have written in your sales letter. Therefore, rather than try to avoid the telephone interview, I recommend that you turn it to your advantage by obtaining information from the PE before going in for the interview.

Handling yourself on the telephone is an important part of your campaign. If a PE wants to interview you by phone, find out all you can about the job before revealing additional information about yourself. If you do give your PE information, make sure it reinforces your credentials for the job.

Sometimes, a PE will want to talk salary over the phone. It is always to your advantage not to do so until a sale has been made. Use this question to obtain more information: "There are so many factors that bear on compensation that it is almost impossible to give you a figure without knowing more about the job. What can you tell me?"

How Roger G. Used the Telephone to His Advantage

Roger G. was a marketing manager for a small plastics firm in New York City. He wanted to relocate to California. In response to one of Roger's sales letters, the vice president of marketing of a San Francisco company called him. "Before we fly you out here, Roger," he said, "we want to know a little more about you." "Certainly," Roger answered. "What kind of marketing manager are you looking for right now?" Roger managed to ask question after question and took three pages of notes before giving the PE specific information about himself. When he did, he was able to tailor his accomplishments to the PE's needs.

The PE was even more impressed with Roger's potential and set up the interview. But Roger didn't stop there. He went over his notes before the interview, carefully organizing his experiences and background to support his qualifications for this job. Naturally, Roger did well in his interview and received an offer at a considerably higher salary than what he had been earning.

● FOLLOWING UP WITH A TELEPHONE CAMPAIGN

A telephone campaign can be very effective for those PEs who do not invite you to interview as a result of your first mailing. In fact, many job seekers find that the results of the telephone campaign a couple weeks after their sales letters are sent nets a better rate of response for interviews than does the initial mailing. There are several likely reasons for this phenomenon. To ask about your letter provides a reason for your call to the PE. Many PEs are on the borderline between inviting you for an interview and not. Placing a call demonstrates your interest and puts them over to your side. Also, some candidates are very persuasive on the phone. Together with the sales letter, this makes for a powerful interview-getting, tool.

If you do decide to follow up by telephone, do not indicate you are going to do so in your letter. It is still better if your PE calls you to request an interview rather than you initiating the call. If you say you are going to follow up with a call, most PEs will not respond to your sales letter. You can use the telephone techniques outlined in Chapter 9.

● WHEN AND HOW TO WRITE THE SECOND SALES LETTER

You should send your second sales letter approximately three weeks after the first. There are several reasons for doing so. Your initial sales letter may not have reached the hiring executive, or business conditions may have changed. An executive can quit, get fired, or be transferred suddenly. An expansion may require greater manpower needs than anticipated. Budget approvals may come through unexpectedly. Sometimes your letter is borderline. Your PE needs just a slight push to get him or her to extend an invitation for an interview. Whatever the reason, your second sales letter may be better received than the first. Finally, a second sales letter helps to establish your credibility that you are "for real." A PE who was on the borderline of responding to your initial sales letter may be convinced by your second letter.

Prepare your second sales letter much like your first, with the following changes: use a different opening/attention getter; and strengthen your "Desire" paragraphs, especially if you did not receive a strong response from your first mailing.

Send your second sales letter to all those PEs who did not invite you for an interview. These include PEs who did not reply at all as well as PEs who sent you a rejection letter, either directly from the hiring executive or from the personnel department. You should also send your second sales letter to additional PEs who have come to your attention since the first mailing. Their names should be on your updated list.

If you are getting good results, you can use your original sales letter with minor changes. However, if your initial mailing brought in poor results, something is wrong with your sales letter (assuming you followed printing and other directions carefully). Reread the early part of this chapter and review the examples. Study every sentence in your sales letter. Sometimes only a small change or omission can make a world of difference. Rewrite your sales letter and send it out again.

● HOW TO KEEP RECORDS OF YOUR SALES LETTER RESULTS

You must keep records of the results of your sales letters so you can determine whether to change your basic sales letter and revise your mailing list for your second letter. You can use your mailing list for your records. To the right of each name draw two columns. Label the first column "Initial Letter" and the second column "Second Letter." As responses come in, put the date in the appropriate column. You can use a code for the type of response: "R" for rejection, "I" for invitation to interview. Always keep all communications and records of communications until your campaign is over.

The Main Point

The best way to get a job fast is by use of a personal sales letter sent *without* a resume.

**ORGANIZE YOUR
ACCOMPLISHMENTS
CHRONOLOGICALLY
IN RESUMES**

7

How to Organize Your Accomplishments for Maximum Impact in Compelling Sales Letters, Faxes, and E-mail

"I was a little leery of using sales letters in the way you recommended. After all, I had been an officer in a major company. How would something like that be viewed? But as I explained to you, I had been out of work for a long time and had tried everything else. Moreover, you had my confidence, so I wrote sales letters and sent them out in the manner you indicated. I wanted to thank you for everything. I am going to be Corporate Vice President responsible for overseas operations in a major corporation."

—A Happy Believer in Your Methods

● THE COPYWRITER'S FORMULA FOR WRITING YOUR SALES LETTER

I have adapted a "secret" formula used by copywriters to help you organize your sales letter in a hard-hitting fashion, for maximum impact with your PE. I call it a secret formula because few job hunters use it, or anything like it. Yet it is a simple adaptation for writing a direct mail sales letter. In this case, the unique product you are "selling" is you. Here it is:

Attention + Interest + Desire + Action = Sales Letter to Get a Great Job Fast

Let's look at each of the elements of this formula in turn. The *Attention* element captures your PE's attention, arouses curiosity, and tempts her to keep reading. The *Interest* part keeps the interest of your PE by explaining why you are writing. Now you add *Desire*. It creates a need for your services by describing what you can do for the PE in a compelling manner. It must also convince your PE of the truth of what you say. Finally, we add *Action*. It makes clear exactly what action the PE should take and subtly suggests that she do it immediately.

● HOW TO GAIN ATTENTION

Your opening/attention getter is the lead paragraph in your sales letter. Your objective here is to get your reader's attention and lead into your purpose for writing. To do this, you can employ news, intrigue, shock, or any kind of unusual information, so long as you can relate it to your basic purpose for writing: to obtain an interview. Here are some examples of successful opening/attention getters:

- "I doubled the work output of my department while cutting engineering man-hours by 25%."

This opening/attention getter was written by Tom J., an engineering manager for a large aerospace company. It was so effective that it got Tom interviews for engineering management jobs in both large companies and small, in several different industries. Tom had to explain in numerous interviews exactly how he did this. Tom's explanation: "Through lack of control, my department was working on unneeded subsystems. I reduced man-hours while doubling productivity on essential work." By the way, note that Tom writes the numbers as "25%" and does not spell it out as "twenty-five percent." Sure, the latter is more correct for English usage. But numbers stand out, and in your sales letter that is exactly what you want them to do.

- "As a professor at the U.S. Military Academy, I taught Juice to Cows who were Goats; 50% of my Goats became Engineers in Juice within 60 days as a direct result of my instruction."

This unusual opening/attention getter was used by Tony B. when he applied for a part-time teaching position at a number of colleges and universities. Tony went on to explain that Juice was slang at the Military Academy for electrical engineering; Cows were college juniors; Goats were cadets with low academic averages; and Engineers were cadets with high academic averages. What Tony was saying was that he taught electrical engineering to juniors with low academic averages, and that 50% of his students achieved high academic averages in electrical engineering as a direct result of his teaching. Few hiring deans could resist reading Tony's sales letter once they had read that opener.

Charlie F., an international commodity salesman, used this opener:

- "I spent 5 years in South America selling $10 million of American coffee in Brazil and other South American countries."

What an attention getter! That's like selling coconuts to natives of a tropical island. You can bet it materially assisted Charlie in getting interviews for a superior job.

Bob G. was a marketing manager with a small government contractor. Bob's opening/attention getter, which eventually led him to a superior job at a 20% increase in salary, told of a single exploit with that company:

- "I captured a $1.5 million government contract from a giant competitor who had done all prior work. This led my small company into an entirely new business grossing $10 million a year."

If you have been accorded special recognition for some business achievement, here is an opening/attention getter that will fit many different situations:

- "Perhaps only once in a lifetime career as a _____ does a man (or woman) have the opportunity to participate in an event so unique as to warrant special recognition and acclaim. Not long ago I was one of the fortunate, I was commended for _____."

All good attention getters have one thing in common: they capture the PE's attention at the start and compel him or her to read on to discover why you are writing.

● HOW TO WRITE THE INTEREST ELEMENT OF YOUR EQUATION AND WHY IT IS IMPORTANT

Once you have aroused your PE's interest by your opening, you will raise one major question in the PE's mind: Why is this person writing to me? The Interest element will answer this question and will encourage the PE to read on. Here are some sample explanations for your sales letter:

- "I am writing to you because you may be in need of someone with my train- ing and experience as a marketing manager. If so, you may be interested in some of my other accomplishments."
- "I write this letter to inquire about your needs for a financial specialist. If you have such a requirement, here are some other things I have done."
- "I am writing to determine if you have a need for someone with my capa- bilities as a salesperson. If you do, you may be interested in additional de- tails of my experience."
- "I am corresponding with you directly in case you need someone with my qualifications as a general manager. Here are some of my other accomplish- ments."
- "Your company may be in need of a vice president of engineering, and therefore may be interested in additional facts about my expertise in this function."
- "I am writing to alert you to my availability as a business development spe- cialist. Here are some of my other accomplishments in this field."

The Interest element of your superior sales letter equation is critical. In ad- dition to telling your PE why you are writing, you will be stating the specific job position you want. Your entire sales letter from Attention to Action must be built around that specific job. As I have mentioned before, many job hunters fail to focus their campaign on a specific job, often because they are afraid of missing out on another job that may be available. As a result, they write something like this: "I am writing in case you need someone with my qualifications for any po- sition that might hold interest for me where I can make a contribution."

Don't make this mistake. You will seriously weaken your chances of getting a face-to-face interview. Instead of presenting yourself as a uniquely qualified individual with an outstanding background for the PE's immediate need, you will appear to be a jack-of-all-trades. That's not a compliment in job hunting, even if you do have multiple experience in several fields. Almost every competitor will appear to be more expert than you for the position that is open. Remember that you are superior to all of your competitors in some way. However, it is equally true that every one of your competitors is superior to you in some way as well. You must be perceived to be superior for that single job that the company seeks to fill. The only exception is if the company (and you) are looking for a jack-of-all-trades position. These are rarer than you think. Mention one position and one position only in your sales letter. Concentrate your resources on a single objective. You have only so much space; make every word support the single job that you have already decided you will accept . . . and no other.

This is so important that I want to repeat it. Aiming for a single position works when the "I can do anything" approach does not. This is because you are aiming your sales letters at the precise bull's-eye of PEs who have an immediate need and want to hire someone in your specialty. Failing to be specific can only weaken your image and dampen the impact of your sales letter. Citing your specific job position objective with supporting background and accomplishments will get you high-quality interviews.

● HOW TO CREATE A DESIRE FOR YOUR SERVICES

In the first part of the Desire element of your sales letter your objective is to create a strong desire for your services. You must make your qualifications so attractive that your PE feels compelled to invite you to his or her company for an interview. You will do this by describing outstanding accomplishments, taken from your resume, that support your job objective.

There are two approaches you can take. One is to state what you have accomplished in the function you have decided upon as your objective. Here is an example:

As a missile design engineer, I:

- Patented five separate inventions, all of which reached production.
- Designed more than 140 components of a major guidance subsystem.
- Saved the company more than $5 million in production costs by redesigning a critical gimbal.

- Developed the methodology of computer redesign of old missile components. This saved more than $1 million in design time the first year of operation and is expected to save more than $10 million company wide in three years.
- Authored 7 technical papers published in house and professional journals. Two were presented at professional society meetings, and one was incorporated into the textbook *Missile Design Handbook*.

The other approach is to list similar functions, all of which support the job you are seeking:

- As director of research and development in a small company, I headed the R&D division. In 1 year I built funded research and development from 0 to a sustained level of $1 million *per* year.
- As subsystems manager on a major aircraft project, I was responsible for $50 million in engine subsystems and coordinated the activities of 65 engineers. I prevented a $5 million overrun and a 12-month slippage.
- As program manager of 9 small development programs totaling more than $2 million per year, I was commended by the vice president of engineering for "being on target, on cost, and on schedule while demonstrating exceptional executive ability and decisive leadership."

In developing the "Desire" part of your sales letter, don't be afraid to use the word *I*. Granted, most successes are team efforts, but would you have been the one pointed at had things turned sour? If so, there is no reason not to state your accomplishments in the first-person singular. A job campaign is definitely not the time for modesty; if you don't tell your PE what you did, no one else will.

Always use short, dynamic, action words such as *directed, led, developed, ran,* and *managed*. A thesaurus will be of assistance in choosing the proper words.

Keep your sentences short and to the point. Write objectively and in a hard-hitting manner, with few adjectives. Let the accomplishments speak for themselves. For example, instead of saying, "I increased sales an incredible 200% say "I expanded sales 200%." Rework your sentences until you get them just right. Check all words for spelling. This is best done using a computer spelling checker and then having someone other than yourself read it over. It is difficult to catch your own mistakes.

Don't cite any accomplishment, no matter how great, unless it supports the job you are seeking. For example, if you are looking for a job in finance and also have an outstanding record in market research, do not describe any of your market research accomplishments unless they relate to finance. Try to state every accomplishment in quantitative terms. Instead of saying, "I gave interviews to a large number of journalists," say, "I gave interviews to 27 journalists." Instead of writing, "I cut cost of sales by a huge percentage," write, "I cut cost of sales by 23%." Don't say, "I prevented a major slippage," say, "I prevented a 4-month slippage."

● HOW TO DEVELOP CREDIBILITY WITH YOUR PE

The second part of "Desire" is developing credibility. Your PE must believe what you say in your letter. It is extremely difficult to check on the accomplishments that you claim. If you are like most, you had to stop and calculate these dollars, figures, and percentages especially for your campaign. Further, most companies will not release percentage figures, even if known. Nor will they talk about the specifics of their businesses in quantitative terms with an executive from another company, especially if that company is a competitor. As a result, many of the accomplishments you have so carefully worked out in quantitative terms cannot be checked. Your PE knows this.

How, then, do you establish conviction that everything you said is true? You can do this by stating facts that a PE *can* check. The best way to do this is with your educational qualifications: "I have a BA in journalism from California State University," or "I have a BS (1982) and MS (1994) in business administration from the University of Wisconsin, specializing in marketing." Or "My BS is in mechanical engineering from the Massachusetts Institute of Technology (1979)." Or "I completed my BA in communications at New York University in 1998."

One question that frequently arises is whether you should state your year of graduation. The answer depends on your situation and the kind of job you are seeking. For example, if you are seeking a chief executive officer's position and you are relatively young, you may want to omit the year of your graduation; if you are older, you may want to include it to emphasize the depth of your experience. Before deciding, consider whether your PE would most likely prefer an older or a younger candidate. Any other information that would document your age should be included only if it is in your best interests. Remember, legal or not, this could be a knock-out factor in the mind of your PE. But once you get the interview, it usually won't matter.

Whenever possible, tailor your education to the specific job. If you have an MBA specializing in marketing and are seeking a marketing position, state the specialty. If the position is not in marketing, state only that you have an MBA. If you have a BS in industrial engineering specializing in human engineering, do not state your specialty unless the job you are seeking is related to it. The principle, as always, is to ensure that every bit of information contained in your sales letter supports the single job objective you have chosen.

What if you haven't graduated from college or haven't attended college? Find something else in your background to use. If you have a professional license of one kind or another—CPA, professional engineer, and so on—use it. If you attended a school but did not graduate, state your educational qualifications in this way: "I attended the University of Minnesota (mechanical engineering)." If you attended more than one school without graduating, you can use this format: "I attended Baltimore City College (business administration), the University of Maryland (business administration), and the University of Pennsylvania (business administration and management)."

If you are not a college graduate but feel you must have a degree in order to obtain a great job, you might consider enrolling in one of the many nontraditional institutions across the country or over the internet. These schools are variously called "universities without walls" or "nontraditional colleges." Some are clearly "diploma mills," though few would admit to being in this category. Many are simply what they say . . . nontraditional. They offer nonaccredited degrees—and in some cases even accredited—based to a varying extent on life experiences. In many cases, depending on the school and your experience, you can become a college graduate fairly rapidly.

Some years ago, I contacted the California Board of Education and discovered that California, like many states, has several classes of college-type institutions. The highest is the one we are all familiar with: an institution that has been accredited. Next on the list is an institution that the state has recommended for accreditation, but has not yet been accepted for accreditation by an accrediting body. Then comes the lowest class: the state "empowers" or "authorizes" the institution to grant degrees, but makes no comment on the quality of the education given. At the time of my call, the basic requirement for this legal "empowerment" was incorporation under state laws with $50,000 in educational equipment. Naturally, this figure has probably increased substantially since my inquiry and undoubtedly varies from state to state.

If you are interested in this type of program, check *The Wall Street Journal*, the business section of your local paper, advertisements in airline magazines, the Yellow Pages of your phone book, or the internet. You can also call your state's Board of Education.

I am mentioning these schools primarily because of the relative ease and speed with which they can make you a "college graduate." However, I should also state that in some cases the quality of the education they offer is high, and I recall that no less an institution than Harvard accepted credit-hour transfers from one of these schools several years ago.

The Call to Action

The last element in the formula for a superior sales letter is Action. You must indicate to your PE exactly what you want him or her to do—namely, to invite you in for an interview. Here are several variations:

- "I would be happy to discuss further details of my experience in a personal interview."
- "I am prepared to discuss additional facts concerning my background in a face-to-face interview."
- "Please call me after 5:30 any day for a personal interview."

The Main Point

Use the copywriter's formula of attention, interest, desire, and action to write great sales letters for use by regular mail, fax, or the Internet.

OBEY ALL STATED
REQUIREMENTS IN
WANT ADS

8

How to Develop a Dynamite Response to a Want Ad by Violating Stated Requirements . . . and Even Get Interviews from Job Ads Without Responding to Them

"This is the first time I looked for a job in this country. My English isn't so good. I was expecting a tough time and only an entry-level position at best. Without your system, I am sure that's all I would have got. I only answered three ads. I was surprised. I got three interviews. I accepted an offer with a major bank as senior financial analyst. My husband and I are very, very grateful to you."

—New Immigrant and Senior Financial Analyst

Ad answering, whether in print or cyberspace, is an outstanding means of generating interviews, second only to your sales letter campaign. A major advantage of answering advertisements is that you can be almost certain that a job is available. In addition, the requirements for the job are usually clearly stated, and there is generally sufficient information to give you an idea of whether the job appeals to you.

Unfortunately, answering ads has a major drawback compared with the sales letter. You're going to have competition, and lots of it. The key to beating your competition in answering ads is to orient your response toward exactly what the advertising company has asked for. That is, your experience, qualifications, and accomplishments should so clearly meet the requirements listed in the advertisement that your response is compelling and demands an interview.

To do this you must violate several requirements in most want ads: Do not send a resume. Do not include a salary history. Do talk to individuals that know something about the job before sending any response.

● HOW TO GET INFORMATION THAT ISN'T IN THE AD

In order to respond effectively, you must know as much about the job as possible. In fact, you shouldn't respond to any advertisement until you have obtained as much information as you can, even from sources other than the advertisement itself. To do this, you must contact two individuals in the company by telephone: the HR or personnel manager and the hiring executive.

If the advertisement is not "blind"—that is, if the company name is given—one of these two executives may be listed in the ad. If the hiring executive's name is not given, you should have no trouble obtaining it. First figure out the executive's title from the title of the position that is open. For example, if the advertisement is for a marketing manager, the position will probably report to a vice president or a director of marketing. You can then call the company and ask for the name of its vice president of marketing. Use the same technique to obtain the name of the HR manager—just ask.

● WHAT TO SAY ON THE TELEPHONE

Tell these individuals that you are interested in the job. They may tell you to "just send a resume." Say that you don't have a resume, but have important accomplishments in the field which you feel would make you an outstanding candidate. However, you need to know more in order to respond to their ad intelligently. Explain that you are highly qualified, but your position is sensitive and you need more information before deciding even whether to respond. Use the following checklist (or a modification of it to suit your circumstances) to obtain as much information as possible:

- What is the exact job title?
- Whom does the position report to?
- What specific experience are you looking for?
- What are the most important functional tasks in the job?
- What factors would cause a candidate to be eliminated from consideration for this position?
- Is this a new opening? If not, what happened to the previous occupant?
- Is a degree required? What kind? An advanced degree? An MBA? A technical degree?
- Are there specific problems that you hope the new employee will solve?

Be tactful, friendly, and courteous, but be firm so you can obtain as much information as possible.

Here is one way of starting out after you have gotten through to the HR manager: "George Smith? Good morning, this is Amy Brown. I heard about your requirement for an accountant and I was wondering if I might take a few minutes of your time to discuss the position." Now George Smith is probably reasonably busy. If his ad is any good, he has had quite a few calls, so his initial response may be "It's all in the ad" or "Just send your resume."

It is your job to draw out the HR manager and get him started on your checklist. Tell him one of the more outstanding tidbits in your background to whet his appetite about your qualifications. Then say you want some information before responding. Or tell him that you currently hold a similar position with a competitor; you know he will respect the confidentiality of your resume, but you would like a few questions answered before sending it.

Another technique is to tell the HR manager that a friend of yours who works for a competitor claims that the position is not very good. So even though you are qualified and interested in the job, you want to give him a chance to respond to your friend's criticisms before sending off your resume. Use a little imagination. The important thing is to get the HR manager talking about the job so he will answer your questions.

You may wonder why I have suggested that you call the HR manager and not the hiring-decision manager first. The reason is that the HR manager is *not* the decision-maker. In talking with him first you can afford to make some mistakes, and you will learn a lot more about the job. Then, when you talk with the decision-maker, you will appear more knowledgeable about the job.

After getting as much information as you can, thank the HR manager and revise your checklist for use when talking with the hiring executive. Do *not* ask the HR manager if you can talk with the hiring executive. You are under no obligation to even announce that you are going to do so. Also, it is much better if you do not, since the HR manager will resent your infringement and the hiring executive's potential infringement on what he perceives to be his territory. Also, one of the HR manager's jobs is to prevent job seekers from talking directly with the hiring executive.

When talking with the hiring executive, say something like this: "John Wood? Hello. This is Amy Brown. I spoke earlier this morning with George Smith about the accountant position opening, and it appears that I am pretty well qualified for the job, but I want to ask a couple of questions if I may." Again, if John Wood asks for a resume, tell him you will respond to his ad, but tactfully get him to answer your questions about the job.

When you talk with the hiring executive who is, after all, your PE—be very careful in your approach, but stay alert to opportunities. Remember your objective is not to send out a beautiful resume; it is to get a face-to-face interview. That's the only way you are going to get a job offer. A written response may be a required step on the way to the interview, but you may be able to sidestep it by talking directly with the PE. Few if any of your competitors will have gotten this far.

If the PE begins to interview you on the telephone, describe some of your accomplishments that specifically support what you have learned about the job. Ask if you may come in for an interview to discuss your background further. You lose nothing by asking. If you can skip the resume stage, you will save time and improve your chances of getting hired. Also, once you have talked with the PE, you can send a covering letter and a special resume directly to his attention, as well as to the HR manager . . . if you must send a resume at all.

Do not ask about salary or fringe benefits when speaking with either executive. That is not the purpose of your call, and such questions can cost you both an interview and a job offer.

● HOW TO BREAK "BLIND" ADS

In a "blind" advertisement the hiring company hides behind a box number or some other camouflage so that it cannot be identified. Blind ads are used for a number of reasons. Sometimes a company doesn't want to reveal its needs to a customer. Sometimes a company wants to conceal an expansion from a competitor. A headhunter may use a blind ad if he doesn't want his client to know that he locates some candidates through advertising, or someone may be "testing the market"—in which case there isn't any job opening at all. I have even heard of a blind ad being used deliberately as a setup to trap an employee into responding so as to "prove" his disloyalty to an employer.

Blind ads pose a problem for the job hunter. Regardless of their intent, they must be "broken" in order to identify the hiring company. If you are currently employed, you must do this without revealing your own identity. One technique that headhunters use to break blind ads is to send a mailgram to the blind address. In the message the respondent explains that he meets every requirement for the position, but because of the sensitivity of his current job he cannot respond fully without knowing the name of the hiring company. This is followed by a brief extract of accomplishments that indicates the high quality of the candidate. The respondent gives an alias (or no name at all) plus a phone number and a request to call. In 50 to 75 percent of the cases advertisers will call the candidate and give him the name of the company.

A typical mailgram for this purpose might look like this:

To: *The Wall Street Journal*
Box AD-205

"Very interested in your advertisement for corporate attorney with petroleum experience. I meet all your stated requirements and have a BS in petroleum engineering as well as an LLB. Have worked as corporate attorney for a petroleum exploration and producing company with $500 million in annual sales. The sensitivity of my present position makes it impossible to respond in more detail without knowing your identity. Please call (717) 555-5996 any day after five o'clock."

You can use either your own telephone number or that of a friend. The advantage of using a friend's number is that it will not be familiar should the blind ad represent your own company. The disadvantage of using a friend's number is that you may not be available to speak with the caller. If a friend takes the call, he should get the company's name as well as the name of the caller, job title, and telephone number. If you take the call, find out all you can about the job and ask for an interview. If the advertiser turns out to be your own company, don't panic. Take the number and use any reason you can think of (without identifying yourself) to gracefully get off the phone.

By the way, you can use the same "mailgram" technique to respond to an ad when only an e-mail address has been given over the internet. Just be sure you have taken precautions so that the addressee does not know from whom the e-mail originates.

Another way of breaking a blind ad is simply to call the newspaper or magazine and ask. Some states require that such information be given out if requested. The worst that can happen is that you will be denied this information.

If you are conducting a campaign while employed, never respond to a blind ad without checking to make certain the advertiser is not your own company. Employees have been discharged for "disloyalty" when they inadvertently responded to blind advertisements from their own companies.

With all the difficulty of responding to blind ads, why bother with them at all? There is good reason. Fewer job seekers respond to blind advertisements than to open ones. Therefore, you will generally have less competition. So do not let the fact that an advertisement is blind deter you from responding. And never underestimate the importance of getting as much information as possible before you answer an advertisement.

How Bob F. Won Out Over 300 Competitors

Bob F. responded to an ad for an engineer for the Internal Revenue Service. Two weeks later he called to find out what happened. By the sheerest of accidents the personnel manager was out for lunch and Bob spoke with a secretary who knew all about the job. Because Bob was courteous and tactful, the secretary was willing to spend some time talking with him. She told Bob that the IRS had received more than 300 responses to the advertisement and that none of the respondents appeared to be fully qualified. So the resumes had all been thrown out and they were going to re-advertise the job.

Bob asked the right questions and discovered exactly what the IRS was seeking. He found out a lot of information that was not in the advertisement or was stated incorrectly. For example, the ad required an undergraduate degree in engineering, and asked for a master's degree with management experience. Bob assumed that the IRS wanted a technical master's degree. He had one and had noted it in his resume. However, Bob also had an MBA. He left it out of his resume in fear that he would sound overeducated. From the ad, he thought that the IRS was looking primarily for a skilled engineer. It turned out that the IRS wasn't looking for a graduate degree in engineering at all. The ad was supposed to have read "master's degree in business." Armed with this knowledge, Bob rewrote his qualifications and accomplishments, tailoring them specifically to the IRS requirements. Within a week after sending out this information, Bob was invited in for an interview and was ultimately hired. Of the 300 respondents, he was the only engineer that interviewed. His new boss told him, "Of all the resumes we got, yours was the only one that had what we were looking for." For Bob, learning everything he could about the job before responding (the second time) made the difference between being offered a great job and preparing material for the wastepaper basket.

● HOW TO USE RESPONSE FREQUENCY TO YOUR ADVANTAGE

You should know one additional point of importance in answering ads. There is an established response pattern that seems to hold regardless of time of year, geographical location, type of job, or any other factor. Many executive job hunters rush to respond to an ad within a few days after it appears, thinking that it will put them ahead of their competitors. This is a mistake. When a PE has many responses to read, he may not read them carefully. Even a good response can get lost in the shuffle. Also, the hiring executive tends to cut large numbers of resumes or responses rather severely, reducing, say, 200 responses to only 5 for final consideration. A response arriving later will compete only with other later responses and the few "winners" from the huge early response, not the entire 200.

To minimize the chance of your response being overlooked and to take advantage of the reduced competition, do not respond until one week after the ad appears. Don't be afraid to wait. The chances are very slim that you will miss out within two weeks after the ad appears. Most good positions are not filled immediately. Would you want to hire someone for an important job without seeing all the top people available? If you respond too early, you are more likely to lose out than to get an immediate interview and quick hire. Bob F.'s interview-getting response didn't arrive until almost three weeks after the ad appeared.

● HOW TO DRAFT A SUPERIOR RESPONSE TO ANY ADVERTISEMENT

When you respond to an advertisement, you must aim at a very small target with a rifle, and not with a shotgun. Take the advertisement apart line by line and list every requirement you find. Add to this list the requirements you discover in talking with the personnel manager and the hiring executive. For every requirement, list three to five accomplishments from your resume that support your qualifications. Omit a requirement only if you do not meet it.

In your response, list the requirements in the same order given in the ad, followed by the requirements you have uncovered on your own. If degree requirements are stated in the ad, state your educational accomplishments immediately after that requirement. If degree requirements are not stated, conclude with this information as you did in your sales letter.

Use and organize the information in your response just as you have done for your sales letter. As with the sales letter, the information comes from the same source: your detailed resume that you keep updating.

Always restate each requirement listed in the advertisement as well as the additional requirements you have identified through other sources. Do this because:

- Frequently when large numbers of resumes are received for one position, a screener looks through them to assure that the basic requirements are met. Restating these requirements makes it easier for the screener, who may know nothing about the job at all, to spot and check off your ability to meet each individual job requirement.
- Restating each requirement shows that you understand the problem.
- Restating acts as a checklist for you so that you will not inadvertently omit a requirement.

Make your response to the advertisement on the same fine stationery and printing that you have decided to use for your sales letters, or by e-mail as discussed in the preceding chapter.

● WHY YOU SHOULDN'T RESPOND TO A REQUEST FOR SALARY INFORMATION

An advertisement may ask you to indicate your salary history and/or desired compensation. It is to your advantage not to give out this information until you get to negotiations. At that time you can use it as the situation dictates to negotiate the highest salary possible. Unfortunately, if you fail to give salary information in your response when they ask for it in the ad, you may be eliminated from the competition for an interview. However, if you do list this information, you could be eliminated anyway, for being outside the range that the PE is willing to pay or thinks you should be making now to be eligible for the job. You will also compromise your ability to negotiate for the highest salary possible.

What do you do? You must base your decision on the particular job, your situation, and how strongly the requirement for salary information is stated in the ad. I recommend not giving out salary information, even if requested, until the final stage of your hunt, when you get into negotiations. Also, as I will explain later in this chapter, if your initial response fails to result in an interview, you will write a follow-up letter. If salary information is requested in the ad, you can include it in the follow-up letter. Do not release it otherwise.

If you have a choice between supplying salary history or desired compensation, it is usually better to give desired compensation, unless your salary history is a strong indication of your outstanding track record. However, if you hope for a sizable increase, it is usually better to hold back. Many industries are reluctant to offer large increases, even if it is to their advantage and you are currently underpaid.

I've put some sample advertisements and how they should be handled in Appendix A. Going through these is well worth your time.

● RESPONDING TO ADVERTISEMENTS ON THE INTERNET

With the advent of the internet, there are many new sources of jobs to which you can respond. The principles are the same. Find out additional information before you respond. If there is no phone number, try to get one by using the company's name. If you have to, give a few of your most outstanding accomplishments by e-mail and ask for additional information. Don't fall into the trap of obeying all the rules as stated . . . at least not if you want a great job fast. However, if you use these techniques to respond to jobs listed at various sites on the internet (and you'll find some listed in Appendix B), use the techniques in this chapter to respond to them.

● WHY SALES LETTERS ARE STILL THE BEST WAY OF GETTING INTERVIEWS

If you have read this chapter carefully and worked the exercises successfully, you have become something of an expert in responding to advertisements. The principles you used in answering these ads are the same regardless of industry or profession, or whether you are responding to a position as CEO or your first job after graduating from college. However, sales letters are still your primary means of getting interviews. You should not answer advertisements and forgo sales letters.

Once your sales letter is written and printed, you can probably send out 300 per day. A 3 percent response—not an unusually high rate—will net you nine interviews per day. Of course, you will be limited by the number of PEs who satisfy your job requirements. But 1,000 sales letters should result in at least 30 interviews if you've written your letter properly and followed my other instructions. Of course, if you use e-mail letters, once you get your system set up, you can send out thousands, instantly.

In contrast, if you spend all your time answering ads, at most you can respond to ten per day; your average will be much lower. To be "on target" with your response, you must spend some time gathering additional intelligence and answering each ad individually. If you generate one interview for every ten of your responses, you will be doing extremely well. Remember, your competitors for each ad can number in the hundreds. And even if you could answer ten ads per day, every day, you would be limited by the number of ads for the kind of job you are seeking. As a result, you may average answering only one ad per day or less. So even though the response-to-interview ratio is much higher for advertisements than for sales letters, you are far better off concentrating on sales letters. Get them in the mail, and than you can start answering ads.

With sales letters, you will generate 30 interviews after about two weeks of work. It will take you a full month to get as many interviews by answering advertisements, even assuming you can respond to ten ads per day, every day, and have a 10 percent success rate in getting invited in for interviews. These assumptions are highly unlikely. To get thirty interviews by answering ads will probably take you a good deal longer.

Finally, it is a fact that only 10 to 15 percent of job openings are advertised. This is one reason why advertised positions are so competitive. They are the most visible and are therefore sought after by the majority of job hunters. The remaining 85 to 90 percent of the openings must be reached by some other means, and your main tool is the personal sales letter.

● HOW TO GET INTERVIEWS FROM JOB ADS WITHOUT ANSWERING THEM

This sounds like "mission impossible," but it works. It does requires a little detective work. What you need to do is to find out who your PE is by name using one or more of the techniques described previously. Then, instead of sending a response to the address or e-mail listed, which probably goes to HR, send your sales letter directly to your PE. When you do this, you short-circuit HR and your response does not need to face an HR screening. Moreover, you cut out just about all of your competition. This works well where you have been able to collect a large number of names, and there is little in the job ad beyond a job title for the position. However, you can also call your PE directly, or have someone else do this, using the techniques for telephone interviewing found in the next chapter.

How a Man Became a Vice President of a Major Corporation even Though He Was Out of Work and Had No Experience in the Industry

My West Point classmate, "Ed," had a most unusual background. During his ninth year of military service, his second tour of combat duty ended when he was severely wounded in Vietnam. He spent the next six months in the hospital and then was discharged from the Army. Ed bummed around Europe for a while, ending up in Greece as a sponge fisherman for a year, and then returned to the United States. He enrolled as an MBA student in a western university, and on completion was hired by a small company starting a chain of health food stores. Ed was successful in building this chain for a year or so, then left this operation for one of a series of entrepreneurial activities. At that time he met a young executive of about his own age (he was then in his late thirties) who was the chief financial officer of a major corporation listed by the New York Stock Exchange. This kindred spirit convinced Ed to come aboard as a director of new business development in what was to be his longest stint with a large company up to that time: one and a half years.

This period of relative quiet in Ed's career ended when both he and his friend were fired when they were discovered out gathering proxies and trying to take over the company.

Ed was out of work. He started a number of entrepreneurial activities and wrote a book on entrepreneurship. But, he wanted a job, and he couldn't find one.

It was about that time that I wrote my first book on job-finding based on my experiences as a "headhunter."[1]

Ed bought my book just as his money was beginning to run out. He called me immediately after reading the book, highly excited about the techniques described in it. He said that he had seen a job that he wanted advertised in *The Wall Street Journal* that very day. He asked if he might come to my home to discuss it with me. I agreed.

Ed entered my den with a fragment of a torn piece of *The Wall Street Journal* grasped in his hand. The scrap torn from the newspaper advertised the job Ed wanted: vice president of a division of a major motion picture studio. Needless to say, I was somewhat surprised.

Ed asked whether it was possible for him to obtain this job. Now, the opening was for a vice president of new business development, and Ed had been director of new business development with the only other large company he had been with. Also, new business development implies a certain background of entrepreneurship credentials, in which Ed had substantial experience. However, the chances of his getting this one single great job were very small. I explained to Ed that while it was possible, he faced considerable risk of failure and that perhaps if he wanted to be a vice president of new business development in a major corporation, a mailing to a number of companies might be a better strategy than relying on only this one job opening. However, Ed was not to be deterred, and as his friend I decided to help him.

Clearly, Ed already had a positive mental attitude, and he also had defined his personal professional objective explicitly. What he did have to do, however, was to plan his job campaign, develop a superior resume, and decide on the exact strategy that should be used to approach this job opportunity.

Ed and I spent several hours together going over his background in some detail, establishing all his experiences, and documenting them as accomplishments (as was recommended to you in an earlier chapter). After some probing, we came up with some impressive achievements. For example, he had started up a new concept for a beverage and had already sold 20,000 cases before it was even manufactured. A marketing plan he had developed for the major corporation that he'd worked for had been implemented and had resulted in the company's stock increasing by 300 percent. And, of course, he was co-author of a book on entrepreneurship.

We decided that he would not respond to the advertisement and the personnel manager listed. Instead, I called the major motion picture studio and asked for the name of the president of the appropriate division. I then asked for him, spoke to him myself, and said that I had a friend who had learned about the opening for this particular position as a vice president and wanted to know more. In this way I found out more about what the job required than was revealed in the advertisement. I also described, just as indicated in the chapter on getting an interview through the telephone, some of Ed's outstanding accomplishments. The president of the division, let's call him Steve, agreed that my classmate sounded like a good candidate. However, he also advised me that the hiring was being handled through his personnel manager. I then suggested that Ed send a letter describing his qualifications to Steve with a copy to the personnel manager, Joe.

After my conversation with Steve I called Joe, telling him that I had spoken with his president and that Ed was sending a letter directly to Steve describing his qualifications and that he, Joe, would be receiving a copy. At that time Joe advised me that they had received 500 resumes (not letters) in response to their advertisement so far.

Ed developed his letter, which was written in the format recommended previously in this chapter. It also mentioned my conversation with Steve.

Several weeks later Ed got a call from Joe. He was invited to a preliminary interview. At this point I advised Ed to implement the techniques on how to interview effectively, which he did. You'll get these in Chapter 12. Ed went to extraordinary lengths to find additional information. He used every single contact he had to get additional contacts, not only within the film industry but also within the company, and to learn everything he possibly could about this particular job as well as what would be expected of the vice president for new business development of this division. Ed went to the extent of making telephone calls around the country for information. By the date of the interview he was very well prepared.

This preliminary screening interview was with Joe, the personnel manager. Ed learned that he was one of ten candidates who had been invited to a screening interview, out of more than 800 resumes that had been submitted to Joe for this position. Most had experience in the industry and almost all had been company officers, which Ed had not. Ed's was the only letter and one of the few of the 800 submissions that indicated neither industrial nor company officer experience. Even so, Ed thought that the interview had gone well.

Several weeks later Ed received an additional call. He was one of the five finalists and was invited in to meet various company officers, including his potential boss, Steve. Again, Ed went to extraordinary lengths to prepare, using the additional information he had obtained from Joe during his interview with him. Once more he felt that the interview session had gone well. It had been with four other company officers including his PE, Steve, and with the president of the major motion picture studio itself.

At this point I was removed from the picture, being called to active duty in the Air Force for approximately a month. On my return Ed called me again, saying that twice during my absence he had been called in for further interviews with various executives and that to his knowledge he was still in the running. Furthermore, he had just been called by Joe to come in the following Tuesday. Although Joe hadn't said so, Ed expected that he was going to receive an offer, and he questioned me about what the salary might be. On Tuesday I was teaching at night and so did not return until late. Ed called a few minutes later to announce that he had received the offer and had accepted it.

Now Ed's success or my previous discussion about sales letters does not mean you should not answer advertisements. Ads are an important means of generating interviews, and if you use the techniques outlined in this chapter you can achieve a very respectable success rate. But do not become so enamored of advertisements that you forget that sales letters are the mainstay of your campaign. Sales letters and other means must be used to reach the unadvertised 85 to 90 percent of job openings.

The Main Point

You can get great interviews from advertisements in newspapers, magazines, or over the Internet. However, the competition is fierce. If you want to compete, follow the guidelines in this chapter and do not send resumes or give salary histories.

● NOTES

1. *The Executive's Guide to Finding a Superior Job* (AMACOM, 1978).

NEVER TALK TO A PROSPECTIVE EMPLOYER BY TELEPHONE

9

HOW TO GET INTERVIEWS BY PHONE THAT LEAD TO A GREAT JOB, FAST

"*The telephone campaign worked best for me. When I called I found being forceful and direct, but not egotistical and overbearing worked best. I told them who I was, what I wanted, and the benefits of what I do. Some said yes, some said no. Everyone was friendly. More than one out of every ten that I called invited me to interview.*"

—A Company President

Many experts say you should not allow yourself to be interviewed on the telephone. Some even recommend techniques for avoiding telephone interviews, such as claiming an immediate appointment somewhere else. The reason many believe that telephone interviews should be avoided at all costs is because a telephone interview will not result in a job offer and if you are not careful, it may even cost you the face-to-face interview you need to get a job. Since you have no experience or training with telephone interviews, their solution to this problem, and recommendation to you, is to avoid them like the plague.

● YOU CAN'T AVOID TELEPHONE INTERVIEWS IF YOU WANT A GREAT JOB

The fact is, you will not always be able to avoid telephone interviews. In fact, if you can get an executive to respond immediately after reading your letter, fax, or e-mail by picking up the telephone to call you, that is highly desirable. Moreover, many if not most, PEs will insist on talking to you before setting up a face-to-face interview, especially if they intend to pay transportation and other costs to have you flown to their location for the interview.

Since you will have to talk with at least some PEs on the phone, you should turn the situation to your advantage. Use the telephone interview to obtain as much information as possible about a job before a face-to-face interview and at the same time make the best impression possible. Also, as you will soon see, you can use the telephone to generate interviews. How do you obtain information about a job without getting interviewed yourself? You must control the conversation so that you ask the questions and provide only the information you want to provide, as in your sales letter. Of course, you must do this without appearing to do so. Does this sound like a tough assignment? Maybe, but it's doable if you know how. This chapter will show you how.

● WHAT THE TTP IS AND WHAT IT WILL DO FOR YOU

TTP stands for Telephone Training Program. I call it a training program because it not only represents a source of interviews, but also gives you essential training that you need. Once you have completed the TTP, you will be able to exploit and maximize the number of interviews you can obtain in other ways, to negotiate over the phone, and finally to make the best impression you possibly can before a face-to-face meeting.

The only way to learn to handle yourself over the telephone is to actually do it. The TTP I will outline accomplishes exactly that. You will talk to executives with the authority to hire, and you will present yourself much as you did in the sales letter. Your task is to persuade the executive to invite you in for an interview and to gain as much information about the position as possible. If you become proficient in this technique, you will be able to line up a large number of interviews, as well as significantly increase the number of offers you receive. For the average job hunter, two interviews per day through the TTP is a good number to shoot for.

The TTP should be started as soon as you have your sales letter campaign under way and you have started to respond to advertisements. You should continue the TTP for two to three weeks, or until you have run out of companies in your local area that you might be interested in working for. If you are in a large metropolitan area and an average-size industry, the TTP can probably be continued indefinitely throughout your campaign. As you continue, you will be honing your telephone manner and getting interviews.

The primary source list of companies for your TTP will be the telephone book. Look under your industry in the Yellow Pages, and simply work down the list. If you do this, you will need to get the executive's full name. You can also get this information on line. The Kelsey Group of Princeton, NJ (www.kelseygroup.com) lists the web site addresses for no less than 896 web-based yellow page directories and the list is growing all the time. Here are a few to get you started:

Big Book	www.bigbook.com
Big yellow	www.bigyellow.com
Fast Yellow Pages	www.fastyellowpages.com/toc.html
GTE SuperPages	www.superpages.gte.net
Yellow Pages	www.ndiyp.com
USA OnLine	www.usaol.com
USA World	www.usaworld.com
Yahoo Yellow Pages	www.yp.yahoo.com

● USING TOLL-FREE TELEPHONE NUMBERS TO CONDUCT YOUR CAMPAIGN

If you want to conduct a national campaign, or even an international campaign, without it costing you a cent, get hold of a copy of AT&T's Toll-Free 800 Business

Buyers Directory. It lists several hundred thousand toll-free numbers, by company, and according to industry. To get a directory, call 1-800-426-8686. The current cost is $27.95, but it's worth every penny. By the way, this directory also lists internet addresses. Using toll-free numbers is the only exception to the rule that a campaign by telephone will be more expensive than most other methods of getting through to your PE.

● GETTING THE DECISION-MAKER'S NAME

The quickest and most direct way to get the hiring executive's name is to call the company. Ask the receptionist for the name of the chief buyer, director of sales, or whatever position the one you are looking for would report to. If the receptionist doesn't give you the executive's first name (the most common response will be "That's Mr. Smith"), ask for it. One technique is simply to assume a name and ask, "Is that Mr. *George* Smith?" "No, it's *Gerald* Smith," the receptionist may answer. Fine. Now you have Mr. Smith's first name. You can also ask her if this is what his friends call him. That information can be very useful in getting through the secretary. Another way of getting the executive's name is from a trade directory of the industry or from an executive register such as *Standard & Poor's*. Only after you have the executive's full name should you ask to speak to him.

● HOW TO GET THROUGH TO THE HIRING EXECUTIVE

The first step in getting through to the hiring executive is to get past the executive's secretary. Many job hunters who have no problem getting through a secretary when they must talk to an executive on business have very real problems when they are job hunting. When making a business call you wouldn't stop to think twice about getting through a secretary to an executive. In fact, you would probably feel insulted if the secretary failed to connect you, even if the executive was fairly senior. Unfortunately, this is usually not true when looking for a job. This is due to the fact that you are engaging in an unfamiliar activity. So you may lack confidence and feel uncomfortable with the task of calling.

To overcome this feeling, you must maintain a positive mental attitude and practice the techniques for getting through to the executive outlined in this chapter. Before you can get through the executive's secretary you must find out the executive's full name. Then, when you talk with the secretary, you should ask for the executive by first and last name and give your own full name. Speak with confidence (but not rudeness or arrogance).

If you are employed and have a secretary, you can also ask her to call and to get the executive on the line. This technique makes it relatively easy for you to get through, but is not advisable if you are conducting a campaign in secret.

● AVOIDING THE SECRETARY COMPLETELY

There is one technique you can use to speak with the executive directly, without talking with the secretary. Do not ask to talk to the executive after you have obtained his name from the receptionist. Instead, call several companies and compile a list of executives' names. Then do your calling after five o'clock. By this hour many secretaries, but not their bosses, have headed for home. You can also call before eight o'clock and get the same results. Of course, this will not always work. Some executives will be gone after five and not be in before eight. Also, some secretaries will be at work early or late.

● DEALING WITH THE SECRETARY

Once you have the PE's full name, there are several techniques you can use in dealing with his secretary. If you know what the executive's friends call him, that is, his or her first name, use it along with the last name. If you don't know for sure, use the first and last names that you have. Always speak with confidence and say, "Good morning. Jim Jones calling for Gerald Smith. Would you connect me please?" Give your first and last name and the first and last name of the executive. The only exception to this rule is if you have a title—in which case, use it: "Dr. Jim Jones calling for Gerald Smith." Do not rush. Concentrate on being smooth but authoritative. If you speak in a natural and confident manner, the secretary will rarely hesitate to connect you with the executive.

You should, however, be prepared in case the secretary questions you further. For example, you may be asked what company you represent. Many executives consult from time to time, and consulting makes an excellent screen when lining up interviews through the TTP. If you have consulted and are asked this question, you can answer truthfully, "The Jim Jones Company." or simply say, "Myself."

You may also be asked the subject of the call. The secret is to have this thought through ahead of time. One fairly good, but generalized answer is "Some confidential _____ problems I have to discuss with him." Fill in the blank with his specialty: "sales," "engineering," "accounting," etc. Using his specialty gives the secretary confidence that you've come to the right place. While no executive needs more problems, they must deal with those that fall in their area of responsibility. You may be tempted to indicate that you want to talk about "opportunities." The problem with this approach is that executives have been inundated with sales calls of all types, and the secretaries know it. If you mention you want to talk to the executive about opportunities, the secretary will probably become suspicious and ask you additional questions.

Under no circumstances should you tell the secretary that you are calling about a job. If you do, the secretary will most likely connect you with the personnel or human resources department. If you are asked if you know Mr. Smith, you might answer, "No, but I'm looking forward to meeting him."

There are any number of questions that a secretary could ask—and any number of satisfactory answers you can give. The key is to think these answers out ahead of time. Every situation will be different, but your technique will improve as you get experience with the program.

Always be courteous but firm with secretaries, even if they refuse to connect you with their bosses without knowing the full details. In this case, say something like this: "I'm sorry. I fully understand it is your duty to protect your boss from unwanted calls. However, this matter is highly confidential, and I cannot discuss it. Let me leave my name and number so you can let your boss know that I called and he can return my call."

Occasionally, an experienced secretary will suspect that you are a job hunter and suggest that you speak with the HR manager. Talking to the HR manager at this point is definitely not in your best interests. So tell the secretary courteously but clearly that you have no reason to talk with anyone but Mr. Smith. And remember, you haven't. Only the hiring executive makes the hiring decision, and it may well be that only he knows of the need for someone in your specialty.

Now you finally have the hiring executive on the line. What do you do? Open by saying, "Gerald Smith, this is Jim Jones." Then pause. The reason for the pause is to allow a response. Based on the response, you may approach the executive slightly differently. First, some executives are of the "old school." They treat others more formally, and they expect to be treated that way themselves. They will ask, "What can I do for you, Mr. Jones?" Note the "Mister." That's a cue that you should address Gerald Smith as "Mr. Smith," or by another title such as "doctor" if you know the person holds that title. On the other hand, the executive may reply more informally: "What can I do for you, Jim?" That's a cue that you should address him by his first name as well.

Some executives write one name, but are called by a different name. For example, my name is William A. Cohen, but my friends call me Bill. When a stranger calls me on the telephone and attempts to get on a first name basis by calling me "William," I am instantly on guard. So the pause also allows time for the executive to say something like, "Actually most people call me Jerry."

As soon as you know how to address the individual you are calling, go into the attention getter as in your sales letter. Follow the items in your sales letter exactly, stopping only to answer questions if you are asked. However, do not read your sales letter. You will sound too stilted. Make an outline of the sales letter and go over each point in turn: attention, interest, desire (three to five points), and action.

After your opening, you can continue to talk on a first-name basis, or go into a first-name basis if the executive seems to have given you cues or permission to do so. This is a judgment call, but getting on a first-name basis, if you can, will add a friendly tone to your conversation and will usually make it easier to get an interview.

When you have finished the attention part of your sales letter, pause. Then say, "I am calling because you may need someone with my capabilities as a . . . . If so, you may be interested in some of my other accomplishments." Pause again.

At this point the PE will generally indicate his interest or lack of it. Do not try to rush through your presentation in the hopes that the PE will allow you to continue talking. Speak slowly and clearly and give the PE a chance to understand what you are saying. The fact is, even if you give a flawless presentation, only a small percentage of executives will need someone with your background. If you deliver your attention getter and explanation clearly, and if the PE needs an executive with your credentials, he will be eager to hear what you have to say. If the PE expresses no interest (and remember the majority of PEs will not be interested; you are after the small percentage who are), thank him for his time and go on to the next name on your list.

Some PEs will ask you to send a resume. You should avoid doing so if possible. Sending the PE a resume before you have had an opportunity to learn everything you can about the position and to develop a special resume for it will waste time and could cost you an interview.

There are several ways of handling this. You can tell the PE that your resume is too general or that you cannot send it because of security reasons (you are presently employed). Your dialogue might go something like this: "Frankly, since I am currently employed, I won't send out my resume until there is mutual interest. But I'll be happy to answer any questions now or in a face-to-face interview. Would that be okay?" Or you can say that you don't have a resume and then ask, "What specifically would you like to know about me?" You can also handle the problem with a question: "What kind of experience should I have?" As a last line of defense, ask if you can bring your resume with you to the interview. The major advantage here is that the interview can result in a job offer, whereas the resume by itself cannot.

● QUESTIONS YOU MUST ASK BEFORE THE INTERVIEW

Before you interview as a result of a telephone solicitation, there are some questions you should ask. If the executive insists on having a resume before seeing you, you will also need to have these questions answered, in order to prepare a special resume. Asking about the kind of experience you should have is a good technique. You can use it to lead into a number of other questions about the job:

- What is the job title?
- Whom does the position report to?
- What specific experience or accomplishments are you looking for?
- What are the most important functional tasks of the job?
- Are there any factors that would definitely eliminate a candidate from this position, such as too much experience in a certain area, or not enough?

Do not ask questions about promotion, fringe benefits, or salary. But do probe tactfully for as much information as possible, and take notes while the PE is talking so you can evaluate each requirement against your own background and accomplishments. Then, even if you must send in a resume, you can slant your experience to the PE's needs.

● HOW TO SCHEDULE AN INTERVIEW BY PHONE

After following the outline of your sales letter completely and telling your PE about yourself, you must make the call to action. If the PE appears interested during your presentation, you can conclude with something like this: "I can tell you are interested in getting together. When would be the best time for me to come in for an interview Monday or Wednesday?"

If the PE appears hesitant, see if you can find out why. Sometimes the best way is the most direct: ask. Use the techniques mentioned earlier to avoid sending a general resume, if that is what is holding the PE back. As soon as you have solved the problem, get back to a call to action. Remember, the purpose of the TTP is to obtain an interview. It is your responsibility to guide the PE along this path and show him exactly what you want him to do: invite you in for an interview.

● THE LIMITATIONS OF GETTING INTERVIEWS BY TELEPHONE

Although the telephone is a good way of getting interviews, it is not the best way. There are two big limitations to this method. First, as with sales letters, only a very small percentage of the PEs you contact will be looking for someone with your background. It can be very discouraging to make call after call and receive rejection after rejection while you search for that tiny percentage of PEs. Second, telephone calls are expensive. Unless you have access to a WATS line, or are taking advantage of a toll-free number, you will not be able to reach out-of-town PEs by telephone without some expense. So the TTP is limited geographically.

Despite these limitations, the TTP is essential to your campaign. If you have integrated the different methods of generating interviews into your campaign plan as recommended, you should always be working on some part of your campaign. The TTP is a means of generating interviews when you are not doing anything else. Also, as with sales letters, you will ferret out jobs that are not advertised.

During the first two weeks of your TTP, when you are spending concentrated time on it, you will generate one to three interviews per day. Equally important, you will learn how to speak with executives on the phone and how to gain and maintain control of your conversations. This is vital for getting interviews that you have initiated through sales letters and responses to advertisements, since most replies will come by telephone. Every day you spend on the TTP will help you sharpen your skills on the telephone. You will be less nervous and more confident about speaking with strangers and persuading them to invite you in for an interview.

● ADDITIONAL HINTS FOR IMPROVING YOUR TELEPHONE TECHNIQUE

Whenever you speak with a PE on the telephone, make sure that you listen. If you ask a question, listen for an answer. If you ask a question and the PE struggles for an answer, or there is dead silence, wait. Let the PE answer. Don't jump in to fill the silence and try to help the PE answer the question. The PE is thinking. Give him time. By listening you will learn a great deal. By answering the question for the PE you will learn nothing.

Regardless of your source for companies to call, do not be concerned if you call some of the same executives to whom you have already sent a sales letter. If they have seen your letter and have decided to invite you in, they will say so. If they have decided not to invite you in, you have nothing to lose by calling. What if your sales letter has not arrived by the time you call? If you make a successful presentation by phone, the arrival of your letter will not hurt you. If you did not get an interview by telephone, your sales letter can only increase your chances of getting one.

Always avoid discussions of salary, even if this subject is raised by the PE. You will find advice on how to control salary discussions in Chapter 10. The basic reason for delaying salary negotiations is that the compensation figure you cite may be too high or too low. If it is too high, the PE may eliminate you because he does not intend to pay that much. Yet a PE may offer far more than he intended after he becomes sold on someone during the interview. If the figure cited is too low, the PE may feel that you don't have enough stature for the job. Also, you may find that you wish to raise your salary objectives when you understand more about the job.

Never indicate that you are desperate or anxious for a job, even if you are. If the PE is hesitant about inviting you in for an interview or insists on seeing a resume first, tell him that you would like to save time by bringing the resume in with you. Then explain that you already have an offer and must make a decision within five working days. You would like to meet the PE and see his company, but you don't want to lose a good offer in order to do this.

PEs prefer executives who are in demand and those whom other companies want. There are real psychological reasons for this. Which would probably interest you more in a romantic partner—someone many others found desirable also, or someone no one else desired? This has nothing to do with reality, only the perception of it. Make certain that the PE perceives that you are in demand.

During your job hunt you will not be able to avoid numerous conversations with PEs by telephone. The TTP will not only get you interviews; it will help you master the art of handling job-hunting situations on the telephone. If you have lost interviews because of your telephone technique in the past, the TTP will ensure that you do not have this problem again.

Finally, before you get on the phone to practice the TTP, get on a dummy phone and practice all of the techniques while role-playing with a friend or relative. Do this 10, 20, or 30 times until your partner says, "You've got it . . . you know how to handle yourself on the phone." If you really want to make this role playing realistic, set it up ahead of time and practice by calling someone over a real phone.

The Main Point

You will need to learn to become proficient at telephone interviewing . . . That's part of finding a great job fast. You can learn how to handle yourself over the telephone and get job-getting interviews at the same time through the TTP.

NEVER ADVERTISE OR PROMOTE YOURSELF

10

How to Shamelessly Advertise and Promote Yourself

"I remember you," he said. "You were the guy who spoke to our management club last December. You were terrific." I could tell right away that I was going to get an offer, and I did."

—A new Vice President of Sales

Pick up any newspaper or trade magazine and you will see numerous advertisements placed by job hunters, usually in the classified section under "Situations Wanted." Despite such widespread advertising, classified ads are not a primary means of obtaining interviews and probably won't get you any interviews at all. The reason is that few PEs will read your "Situations Wanted" advertisement. As explained earlier, the same is true for ads placed on the internet, no matter how many billions of prospective employers you are exposed to. So, you are not reaching the market for your services, and your chances of connecting with a PE who is looking for someone with your qualifications are pretty slim. Even a big flashy display advertisement is expensive and may not be cost-effective compared with other means of securing interviews. Moreover, in some print media, you may face a one or two month delay before the ad appears.

However, advertising can be a useful adjunct to your campaign. To maximize the returns from your ad, you must know where to advertise, what type of advertisement to place, and how to construct your advertisement for maximum effect.

If you place an advertisement in a general circulation magazine or newspaper, the only responses you receive may be prospectuses from firms eager to assist you (for a fee) with job-hunting services. In order to advertise effectively, you must select publications that your PEs are likely to read—business papers, trade magazines, professional journals, and so on. Once you have selected the best publications, check to see when your ad will appear so that you can allow for the lead-time in your campaign.

● WHAT TYPE OF ADVERTISEMENT TO PLACE

Few PEs take the time to read down a list of classified advertisements on the off-chance that they will find an employee they are seeking. A PE may, however, respond to a well-written advertisement if he or she sees it. The only way to ensure that a PE sees your ad is to use a display advertisement—that is, one that catches his eye because it has been set in a different type size and style than the usual ads. It may be artistically prepared, with different sizes of type. It is at least one column wide and at least one inch high. Such an advertisement can cost several hundred dollars or more, depending on the paper or magazine and how many times you run the ad.

● HOW TO CONSTRUCT YOUR ADVERTISEMENT

Your advertisement should be an abbreviated version of your sales letter, with the same purpose in mind: to get the interview. The basic parts of your advertisement are Attention, Interest, Desire, and Action. Sound familiar? Right, it is the same formula we used for the sales letter. The basics are the same. Our only change is how we present the material.

● ATTENTION AND INTEREST

For the attention element, use a headline. The objective of the headline is to attract the PE's attention and encourage him to keep reading. It serves the same function as the attention getter and the interest element in your sales letter. Your headline should be short and to the point. Make every word count. You are aiming at the PE who has a need for your services and happens to be glancing through the medium you are advertising in. If your headline captures his attention, he will read the rest of your ad. Here are some examples of headlines:

"Marketing Executive Opened $50 Million Segment—Available"

"Electronics R&D Manager Directed Development of 76 New Products—Looking for New Opportunities"

"'Girl Wonder'—Developed 7 Marketing Plans While a Student—Seeking Great Job"

● DESIRE

Like your sales letter, the desire part gives compelling reasons for someone to hire you. Rework the statements of accomplishment in your letter, eliminating titles and personal pronouns. Keep the action words and the quantitative descriptions. Your presentation should list no more than five accomplishments. Here are some examples:

- "Developed strategies that boosted sales from $5 million to $10 million in 2 years."
- "Found 7 new markets for 3 old products for $3 million in profit."

- "Turned a loss product into the leading product in 3 months."
- "Completed marketing research study with $5 million potential."

Use your educational background to insure credibility, just as you did in your sales letter. Again, eliminate personal pronouns and unnecessary words. For example: "BA and MBA specializing in marketing, University of Colorado."

● ACTION

Again, as with your sales letter, you must call your PE to action. Never omit the call to action when placing an advertisement. Combine your call to action with your address by saying, "Write Box XYZ, *Aviation Week*," or "Call (713) 555-4986." You should list a box number or a telephone number in order to keep your identity confidential until the PE has contacted you. Use a telephone number if possible, since many PEs prefer to respond by phone. Of course, there is nothing wrong with listing a box number as well. If you want to personalize your ad, use your first name: "Call Bob at (713) 555-4986."

● WHAT TO DO IF YOU MUST CONDUCT YOUR CAMPAIGN IN SECRET

If your campaign is to be conducted in secret, you must be very careful in preparing your advertisement. You may have to list a friend's telephone number or use an answering service. To be completely safe, you may not want to list even an area code, since this small clue could give away your identity when combined with other information in your advertisement. State your college degrees but do not give your school or schools. Be careful not to mention any unusual accomplishments or assignments that could allow a business acquaintance to identify you. If you are looking for a great job in secret, you can advertise, but you must be extremely careful. Be sure to read Chapter 11.

● FIVE VERY EFFECTIVE WAYS TO ADVERTISE YOURSELF INDIRECTLY

In addition to the method described above, there are five ways that are extremely effective for advertising yourself and promoting your expertise in any field or for any job. These are:

- Writing articles
- Making speeches and giving seminars
- Maintaining active memberships in organizations
- Initiating your own publicity releases
- Presenting papers at professional meetings

All these methods mean direct exposure for you, and exposure means career contacts in two ways. First, it will bring you to the attention of various headhunters who are seeking to fill positions. This is not a short-term thing. You cannot expect to become active in an organization, and get a job offer a couple days later. However, over the long term, your name will become known. When someone of your qualifications and with your expertise is sought, you are much more likely to be called by headhunters or companies that are seeking to fill top-level positions in your field.

Secondly, the exposure given to you by these five methods means personal contact with people who will see you perform as an expert or will observe what you have done in writing, in public speaking, or in some other way. These contacts can be used by you during your search.

Not only have I seen others use these methods effectively, I've been contacted and offered various positions because of my activity in all five of the above areas. You can do the same thing.

Now, let's look at each method in detail to see how it is used.

● WRITING ARTICLES

If you have the ability to write, writing articles is an excellent means to obtain publicity, exposure, and eventual job offers. The topic that you select to write about is important. It must be relevant to your work. It could be an opinion about the best way to do things, a special technique or some method you have developed or adopted, or even a survey pertaining to your field. Some journals prefer shorter articles, some more extensive ones. *Writer's Market,* published annually by Writer's Digest Books, 1507 Dana Ave, Cincinnati, Ohio 45207 will give you a list of publications that may be interested in publishing an article written by you. You can probably find a copy in your local library.

It is important that you write for the correct audience. Therefore, you should read very closely the description each publication gives of its readership. You want to write for a group of executives who have the authority to hire you.

Therefore, writing for a general or an academic publication usually will be of little help. It is also important that your article be slanted for this readership. Before you begin to write, it would be a good idea to obtain a copy of the magazine that you intend to target.

The biographical sketch of yourself that you send with your article should identify you with the company that you are currently working for. It should also include other items in your background that will establish your expertise for writing the article. Remember, these things may interest PEs as well.

● MAKING SPEECHES AND GIVING SEMINARS

Making speeches in your area of expertise is an excellent way of becoming well known as an expert in your industry and specialty and as a potential high-powered performer for any company. It is also a very easy way to publicize yourself, since there are many more organizations that need speakers for their luncheon, supper, or other meetings than there are speakers available to do the job. If you line yourself up for only one speech a week, and even if the group you address numbers only 20 people, in a year you will have made over 1,000 contacts who will recognize you as an expert in your field.

What subject should you speak on? Choose a subject that can demonstrate your expertise and that will interest as large a group as possible. For example, if you are an accountant and have some expertise on a certain aspect of corporate accounting such as corporate tax laws or how to accomplish zero-base budgeting, this may be a good area to speak on. If you are an engineer and have knowledge about design engineering, quality control, or some other technical area, this too may be of great interest to various groups.

Many new graduates are afraid to try this. They think they are too young and too inexperienced. They short-change the knowledge they acquired through their years at college. Yet, because new discoveries are being made all the time, any recent graduate will have learned much that is not known by a PE. In fact, you can learn much from reading without even attending college. Perhaps you've seen Anthony Robbins on one of his television advertisements? His successful infomercial advertising his tapes on personal power is still running though it started more than ten years ago. Robbins made millions from what he teaches to his students . . . and many of his students are PhDs and top corporate executives. Yet Robbins himself never even attended college. He started speaking on topics on which he had gained expertise while he was still in his teens. He has been giving his seminars since he was in his early twenties.

He says he acquired his knowledge from reading more than 700 books and attending seminars himself. An undergraduate in engineering I know started giving speeches and within two years of graduation was conducting paid seminars for medical doctors. Another student from my university started giving paid seminars to corporations and the government on strategic planning and other management issues before she even graduated. What others can do, you can do.

Speeches may vary in length from 15 minutes to as long as an hour. Prepare the outline of a presentation that will allow you to go either way. You can then either shorten or lengthen your speech according to the occasion. This way, you can address many more organizations than you could if you simply had a single speech of a set length.

Your next step is to find organizations that would like to have you speak. As I mentioned previously, many organizations have monthly meetings and are eager to invite speakers on subjects that will interest their membership. One way of locating such organizations is simply to use the Yellow Pages of your telephone book and look under "Associations." Call every single association listed. Tell them all that you are an expert in your particular area and that you would be willing to give them a free presentation on this subject. If they ask how long the presentation would be, tell them you would be happy to tailor it from 15 minutes to an hour depending on their needs. They will then tell you exactly what their needs are. Be sure to think of some highlights to mention on the telephone that not only show that you know what you're talking about but also demonstrate that the subject would be of interest to a prospective audience.

You may also find groups to speak to by calling up major companies and asking whether they have a manager's club. If they do, the club will have a president, a secretary, or someone in charge of entertainment. Many major companies have management clubs, and as many as several hundred or more people may attend each event. What a great way to make contacts who may turn out to be prospective employers later on down the line!

A third way to make contacts for speeches is to go to your library and look at a book called *Encyclopedia of Associations*. This lists every major association in the United States. You can write a short letter to those that are not in your local area, telling them about your speech and the fact that you are offering to make such a speech to their organization. A short, direct mail sales letter like those used for finding a job can easily bring you a number of different engagements.

As with writing articles, a fringe benefit of making speeches is that in many cases you will be paid for your presentation.

Sharing your expertise with others through seminars is an excellent way of promoting yourself, becoming well-known, and gaining the exposure that will lead to outstanding career contacts. Seminars are not much different from speeches, except that they may be a little longer. Usually anything less than two hours is called a speech, more than that, a seminar. There are several ways of doing seminars.

One is setting up your own seminar, writing all the promotional material yourself, and paying for the printing, the rental of mailing lists, and other expense. You do the entire project as an entrepreneur. Like Tony Robbins, many individuals do this full time and earn substantial financial rewards for their efforts. A thousand dollars or more per day is not unusual. In fact, one very well-known seminar company started in exactly this fashion, with a government employee using his annual two-week vacation to give seminars on government contracting. Eventually he left government employment to do this on his own, year round, and today this same company has trained thousands of people in industry interested in doing business with the government. However, doing everything as an entrepreneur requires a great deal of effort, and if your primary purpose is to seek career contacts for finding a superior job, it is not the most efficient way of getting this accomplished.

There are alternative ways that are much easier. One is to go to local universities and colleges in your area and contact their continuing education department. Almost every college and university in the United States today has a program of educating executives through various seminars. In some cases, these seminars are taught by faculty from the university. Many, many others are taught by individuals like yourself who have expertise in some area gained either through study or personal experience.

A third way to start giving seminars is to contact organizations that specifically give seminars to executives. One example of this is the American Management Association, which conducts seminars and courses all over the country on a continuing basis. Write to American Management Associations, 135 West 50th Street, New York, New York 10020, and ask for their current course catalog. From this catalog you will see various types of courses that are available. You may then contact the person in charge of the specific functional area you are interested in and volunteer to give a course in the area noted.

● ACTIVE MEMBERSHIPS IN ORGANIZATIONS

Being an active member in a number of organizations is another great way to gain exposure for career contacts. However, active membership means exactly that. It means you cannot just join an organization, but should go to its functions and, if possible, become an officer. These organizations may be professional such as the American Marketing Association, which has local chapters all over the country. They could be related to the college or university from which you graduated, or they could even be social organizations of one type or another. All these are outstanding opportunities to make contacts. Even in an athletic club it would be unusual not to make friends and to know who is doing what. If you have the opportunity to become an officer in the organization, you can then demonstrate your leadership and management skills. Whenever you may need a new position in the future, you have the contacts ready and waiting who are already aware of your abilities.

● INITIATING YOUR OWN PUBLICITY RELEASES

Every major firm and a number of knowledgeable smaller firms give publicity releases to newspapers, interested magazines, and other publications whenever they can. This publicity usually results in additional business for them.

In the same way, you can initiate your own publicity releases for whenever you do something. This will demonstrate your ability, make you look good to your present boss, and also get you noticed by others in your field, who may then regard you as an expert. Now, you may be thinking, how can I give a publicity release on anything if I am working for a company that handles publicity itself? Most companies have a publicity department or at least someone handling this task. You may be able to persuade your company's publicity department to do an occasional release. This helps the company as well. But remember, the company's purpose is different from yours. The company's objective is to publicize the company, not to provide the personal publicity you are going to use to help you get a great job. Therefore, you shouldn't depend on your company's publicity department entirely, but should send out your own releases whenever something happens to you or you have something to say that (1) demonstrates expertise and (2) may be of interest to someone and would therefore be published by a newspaper, magazine, or journal of your industry.

What might the topics of such publicity releases be? Well, for one thing, if you succeeded in publishing an article or giving a speech, you might want to publicize something you said or wrote about if it is of interest to other people in your industry. You can then indicate that this was said during such and such a speech or in such and such an article. This publicity will expand your opportunities for additional speeches and articles, as well as expose you to opportunities for a superior job. If you are doing something outside of work that has nothing to do with your current job but is in the same field, publicity here will help you also. Perhaps you are an engineer and have designed something outside of work that does not interest your own company. A publicity release under these circumstances is perfectly legitimate, and it will gain publicity not only for your invention, but also for your expertise. At the same time, it won't offend the company that you are currently working for.

Writing a publicity release is not difficult. You simply write at the top of the page "For Immediate Release" and then go on to describe whatever it is that has happened that you wish to have publicity on. If you have a photograph of yourself to include with the release, this can sometimes be printed as well and will definitely help to publicize you and make more people read the release.

If you wish, you may use a cover letter with the publicity release, addressed to the editor of the magazine or newspaper, or the editor of the department in which you are seeking publicity. However, this isn't strictly necessary. A publicity release by itself can be extremely effective as a single enclosure.

How do you know where to send your publicity release? One excellent source is *Standard Rate and Data Service* (or *SRDS*), which publishes a number of different directories periodically and can be found in your library. These include directories of business magazines, consumer magazines, and newspapers. There are literally thousands of publications available, so, again, you must seek your target market and send the publicity release only to those that serve your target audience of PEs who may be interested in hiring you at some time in the future.

● PRESENTING PAPERS AT PROFESSIONAL MEETINGS

Even attendance at professional meetings can boost your career, since it in itself is a method of exposure and contact with others who may have the power to give you the great job that you seek. However, a far better way is to present a paper at such a meeting, since, again, this establishes your expertise and also exposes you to many more people through your presentation than you would meet in the normal course of events at a conference or professional meeting. This is both a long-range and a short-range proposition. In many cases you can actually meet contacts immediately interested in hiring you for various positions. For the long range, many executive recruiters use conference papers and lists of attendees as sources for potential candidates for positions they are seeking to fill.

The Main Point

Advertising yourself should be only an adjunct to your main campaign. But such a campaign can be an effective adjunct if you advertise in media that prospects are likely to read; make your ad a display ad, in effect, a mini-sales letter; and use all five long-term means of advertising long before you need a job.

BREAK THE RULE

YOU CAN'T LOOK FOR A JOB WITHOUT SOMEONE KNOWING

11

HOW TO FIND A GREAT JOB IN SECRET

"You got offered how much from who? My former boss almost fell out of his plush, highly padded, leather seat. He immediately made a counter offer. He should have been paying me that a long time ago. I turned him down."

—A successful job hunter

As a rule, it is better to look for a new job while you are still employed in your old one. Being employed while job hunting has definite advantages. You are under no time pressure or financial pressure, and you are generally more attractive to a PE than an unemployed candidate.

The main disadvantage of job hunting while employed is the need to conduct your campaign in secret. If your present employer finds out that you are looking, you can lose any chance for a promotion or raise and you may even be fired. Unfortunately, the secrecy requirement makes it difficult *or* impossible to use some of the techniques discussed in this book. It will also lengthen your job campaign. But, it doesn't mean you can't do it. You can find a great job in secret.

The basic principles outlined in this book will help any job hunter find a superior job. This chapter will focus on the changes you must make if you are employed and must conduct your campaign in secret. The techniques described will increase your security at your present job and help you to perform your duties adequately while job hunting.

● HOW TO REORIENT YOUR SALES LETTER CAMPAIGN

Depending on your job level and other factors, it may not be wise to distribute sales letters through your industry, since your present employer could learn of your campaign. To get around this problem, you can use the third-party technique. Write your sales letter so that it appears to describe someone else, not you. For example, in your attention getter do not say, "I turned a $500,000 loss situation into a profit within six months." Instead say, "I know an executive who turned a $500,000 loss situation into a profit within six months." For your explanation paragraph say something like this: "If you need a general manager, you may be interested in some of this executive's other accomplishments."

In the "desire" part of your letter, describe your accomplishments just as you would in a sales letter. Change the credibility paragraph to read something like this: "This individual has a BS in engineering from Iowa State University and an MBA specializing in finance from the University of Illinois." In the call to action say, "If you would like further details, call or write the undersigned, who will arrange a personal interview."

● WHAT TO DO WHEN YOU ARE CONTACTED BY THE PE

When you are contacted by the PE, reveal yourself as the job candidate only after the PE is committed to an interview. If you have any doubts about the authenticity of the call, don't reveal yourself until the interview or until you have enough time to investigate the company.

Obviously, this method is hardly foolproof; and if your present employer gets hold of your sales letter, whether in print or e-mail, it will be obvious just who you are fronting for. However, the third-party approach does allow for an element of doubt and makes it more difficult for your present employer to take punitive action against you. It also has the advantage of being more objective than a first-person letter, since it appears that someone else is commending you rather than you saying good things about yourself.

● WHO SHOULD SIGN YOUR THIRD-PARTY SALES LETTER?

Depending on your situation and the resources available to you, you may not want to sign a third-party sales letter yourself. You can increase security by having a friend act as your front. Your friend would sign the sales letter, take telephone calls, and set up interviews for you. If you use this method, you need not admit deception, as you must eventually do if you sign the letter yourself. Also, there is less chance that your employer will find out about your job campaign. Naturally, if whoever signs the letter is someone well known or important, such as a senior corporate officer, this will increase your response rate.

Tell whoever signs your letter exactly what to say on the phone and what questions to ask the PE. Naturally, you want to get as much information as possible so that you can decide how to handle the situation when you call the PE.

If your campaign is to be conducted in secret, use the third-party sales letter in writing to headhunters. After a headhunter calls you, reveal your identity only if the recruiter and his modus operandi sound right. If the executive recruiter has no specific assignment for you, make certain he understands that you do not want any information on your background distributed to his clients.

Most executive recruiters are ethical. They realize the extreme confidentiality of the information you give them and will not release any information that could get back to your present employer. However, it is wise to stress to any headhunter that you are presently employed and that the information you provide is sensitive. Remember also that there are all kinds of headhunters, so you must be cautious.

● HOW TO RESPOND TO A "BLIND" ADVERTISEMENT

One of the most difficult tasks in a secret job campaign is answering a "blind" ad. Responding executives are often horrified to discover that what appeared to be a truly outstanding opportunity was a job at their level or lower in their own company. Imaginative personnel managers can do wonders with the most prosaic of jobs. Employees who blissfully respond with little caution or forethought are needlessly risking their present jobs.

You should respond to blind ads that hold interest for you. As mentioned previously, blind ads usually generate fewer total responses than open ads, since many employed job hunters are reluctant to use them. Thus a significant portion of your competition is eliminated before you even pick up your pen.

Before responding to the blind ad, you must discover who is behind it without revealing your own identity. Some methods of concealing your identity while breaking a blind advertisement have been discussed in previous chapters.

Another technique you can use is a variation of the third-party approach. As in the third-party sales letter, begin your response with "I have a friend who . . ." or "I know an executive who . . . ." Then lead into a special explanation: "I am writing to you in response to your advertisement for an advertising manager. However, because this individual is currently employed, he does not wish to reveal his identity until your identity has been established." Take the advertisement apart as discussed in Chapter 9 listing each requirement and describing specific accomplishments that qualify you for the job. Your concluding paragraph should read along these lines: "This individual will be happy to meet with you to discuss further details of his background and the position. Please contact me at the address or phone number listed in this letter."

Another way to discover the advertiser's identity is to use an answering service at a rented address. In this case, you should write a first-person response to the advertisement, ending with the following sentence: "Because of the sensitivity of my current position, I cannot reveal my identity at this time. Please call or write the answering service listed in this letter." Don't forget to instruct the answering service not to reveal your name to callers.

Finally, you can rent a box number and use that for your address, signing the letter with the box number rather than your name. At the end of the letter explain why you are not revealing your identity and when you will be prepared to do so. The major disadvantage of this method is that it requires the PE to respond in writing. Many PEs prefer to contact prospective employees by telephone. Keep in mind that any method that does not allow a PE to call will cost you a certain number of interviews.

● ADDITIONAL GUIDELINES FOR CONDUCTING A CAMPAIGN IN SECRET

If you are currently employed, it will be difficult to participate in a telephone campaign unless you use vacation time or take time off from your normal routine. However, if you can manage to practice telephone techniques to generate interviews, use the third-party approach. Start your conversation, as in a third-party sales letter, with "I have a friend who . . ." or "I know someone who . . . ." After interest has been established, you can reveal yourself as the job candidate. If a PE requests information by mail, keep your identity secret until an interview is confirmed.

Regardless of what technique you use, you must be extremely careful of what you say about yourself until you are ready to drop your cover. Unusual experiences or assignments can be particularly revealing. You must either omit these items from communications with a PE even though they would add to your presentation or disguise them in such a way as to make them innocuous. For example, if you earned a Ph.D. in Paraguay, don't mention the school or country in describing your education. If you are the only one in your industry who has worked in China, either do not indicate where you obtained your experience or describe it as "experience in the Far East."

In general, you can trust PEs to keep your file confidential. But it takes only one exception—one PE getting back to your current employer—to endanger your security. For this reason, you should make it clear to every PE that you do not want anyone contacted until you have a firm offer. To make sure that your wishes are followed, do not release the names of former employers until you have an offer and are interested in going to work for the PE.

Use descriptions instead of names. For example, if you must fill out an employment form, describe your present company as "a major firm in the garment industry" or "a small independent petroleum company." Do the same with former employers. For your references, write descriptions of their present office or function: "manufacturing manager of a large company" or "past president of the American Bar Association." Finally, note on the application that you will provide names of companies and individuals after mutual interest has been established, and that you do not wish your present employer, references, or anyone else contacted until that time.

The Story of Engineer X

Engineer X was a bright, experienced engineer who once worked for me. He was doing well and as far as I knew was happy with his assignment. One day, out of the blue, I received a form letter from the personnel manager of a large company in the East. The letter stated that Engineer X was being considered for a job and asked me to fill out a detailed questionnaire on his salary, qualifications, and duties and my opinion of his performance.

When I questioned Engineer X, I was surprised to learn he had specifically requested that his present company not be contacted until he had accepted an offer. At the time I received the form letter, no offer had been made. Since I believe that employees are not showing disloyalty by trying to better their job situation and have every right to do so, I took no punitive action. But it is an unpleasant fact that such unauthorized inquiries are made. The burden is on the executive job hunter to take the necessary precautions.

● ADJUSTING THE LENGTH OF YOUR CAMPAIGN

A campaign conducted in secret will take longer than one conducted in the open. Because you are fully occupied during normal working hours, you must spend evenings and weekends on your campaign. Your unemployed competitors have two major advantages. They can spend eight hours *or* more on their campaign every day, and they are highly motivated to get a job as soon as possible. Such a competitor can beat you out of a great job if you are not careful.

But do not be dismayed if you are employed and must conduct your campaign in secret. If you are careful and take the precautions I discussed in this chapter, it is unlikely that your present employer will find out about your search. There is no sadder sight than an unhappy employee who plods along for years in a job he or she detests because of fear of a present employer finding out about a search for another job.

Don't let fear of losing your present position keep you from getting a great job. Take the necessary precautions and work hard on your campaign. If you do, you will be able to find a great job within a reasonable time without jeopardizing your present position.

The Main Point

It is more difficult to run a campaign in secret, but it can be done fairly easily if you are careful and adjust your campaign and the techniques used to allow for its security aspect.

**LET THE INTERVIEWER RUN
THE INTERVIEW**

12

How to Gain and Maintain Control of Every Interview

"I wondered whether your interviewing techniques would work in the hotel industry or for me as a new graduate. They expect you to have a resume and talk about your background a little and then answer questions, not start asking them of your interviewer. If you do ask questions, it's generally expected to be about benefits. I was surprised when the hotel manager seemed to enjoy being interviewed about his hotel. Also, he was impressed with my knowledge about his hotel, the chain, and the industry. I was ready thanks to your words on research. The key is to keep it light and friendly. Anyway, I got the job!"

—A New Assistant Hotel Manager

Almost every job interviewee enters the interview wondering what is going to happen. What will be the procedure? What questions will the interviewer ask? Will I be able to answer them? I am happy to say, that from now on you need wonder no more, because you will control, if not all, then most of the interview. While there may be questions asked, you will be prepared for them. But most important, it will be *you* who will ask the majority of the questions.

● THE INTERVIEW IS THE PAYOFF

The interview is the payoff of all the actions taken thus far in your campaign. Very few job candidates receive a job offer or get hired without an interview for executive and professional jobs, and especially not for great jobs. If you get such a job offer without an interview, I would be highly suspicious. I would do some serious checking before accepting. In this chapter I will show you how to interview successfully, how to control the interview so that it goes your way, and how to come out with a high percentage of job offers.

● TWO IMPORTANT PRINCIPLES OF INTERVIEWING

There are two principles of interviewing that you must obey throughout your campaign. I say *must* obey because if you do not you will lose job offers and prolong your campaign. The first principle is never to turn down an interview. At the interview you may learn additional facts that make the job more attractive to you. Further, your interviewing techniques and overall performance will improve with each interview. The more time you spend interviewing, the better you will perform in the interview situation.

The second principle is to try to get the PE to extend you a job offer, even if you do not want the job. Why? First, you can always turn an offer down after it has been made. But if you don't make an honest effort to get an offer during an interview, you usually cannot get the PE to extend the offer later. Second, if you make a practice of not trying for a job during the interview, you will be developing the wrong attitude. You will not learn how to master all the interviewing skills you need. Practice getting the PE to offer you the job. Then when you find the great job you really want, you will have the skills you need to get the offer.

How Richard C. Got a Great Job He Could Have Lost

Richard C. was an out-of-work dietician. About three weeks into his job campaign he had an outstanding interview for a job as senior dietician. In the meantime Richard was invited for an interview with another company. It, too, was for a good job. Richard was so certain of being offered the first job that he considered telling company number two that he really wasn't interested.

Fortunately, Richard remembered both principles of interviewing. He went into the second interview pretending that the first interview had never taken place, and he went after the second job offer in earnest. It was a good thing that Richard did. Not only did he discover some facts that made the second offer better than the first, but the first job offer failed to materialize. Richard had an immediate backup offer that he accepted. Today, some years later, he is a vice president with company number two.

● WHAT INFORMATION YOU SHOULD GET BEFORE THE INTERVIEW

The interview should begin long before it takes place in person. In fact, it begins with your first contact with the PE. As pointed out in earlier chapters, in your initial telephone conversation you should try to learn as much as you can about the job, the PE, and the individuals you will be working with. If the invitation for the interview comes to you by mail, you must take the initiative and make the telephone contact to get additional information.

Before the face-to-face interview, you should ask the PE for a full description of the position (including why it is available) and a description of the qualities the PE is looking for. You should also find out what happened to the individual who previously held the job, whom the position reports to, and who you will interview with besides the hiring executive.

To get additional information before the interview, talk to anyone in the hiring company who might help. Ask questions casually, as you engage the other party in conversation. Get as much information as you can, but don't push. If the individual refuses to answer a question, give way. Then proceed with some other questions. Always be pleasant and courteous. Do not under any circumstances get into an argument with a representative of the PE, even if you are provoked.

Do not be offended if the hiring executive does not make the initial contact. The hiring executive may be very busy and may ask someone else to call you to schedule an interview or to see if you are worth talking to. Use this opportunity to get all the pre-interview intelligence you can. Frequently you will get valuable information that will assist you during the interview in presenting yourself as that unique candidate who fits all the PE's needs. However, keep in mind that your objective in the initial phone conversation is not to reveal information about yourself; it is to obtain additional information about the job and the PE.

● WHAT TO DO AFTER SETTING UP THE INTERVIEW

After setting up the interview and getting as much information as you can, you should do some research on the company and the executives you will be meeting. One good source is *Standard & Poor's Register* of *Corporations, Directors, and Executives*. Greenwood Press has a four volume reference set entitled *Biographical Dictionary of American Business Leaders* by John N. Ingram. Go to www.amazon.com and www.bn.com for some additional ones. The point is, there are dozens of references that can help you. You don't need to buy any. Just ask your librarian for help.

You can also get information on your PE from your bank or brokerage house, the PE's annual report, *Fortune's* 500 listing, *Moody's Annual, Dun & Bradstreet* directories, a company's 10K report from the Securities and Exchange Commission, and special editions of trade magazines. These include magazines such as *Plastics* for the plastics industry, and *Oil and Gas* for the petroleum industry. You should go through recent editions of trade magazines, *The Wall Street Journal,* and the business sections of major newspapers for changes and developments in a firm.

The internet is great boon to job hunters preparing for interviews because you can find a lot of information on a company, individual executives, and a company's products. All of this can be found on an organization's web site. Moreover, many businesses and magazines such as *The Wall Street Journal, Business Week, Fortune,* and others will allow you to search their archives.

For the executives you are going to meet, you should find out about education and schools, industrial and other experience, hobbies and other aspects of their backgrounds that you may have in common. For the company, you should get information on products, annual sales, recent achievements, recent problems, acquisitions, and divestitures. Most of this information you can get simply by asking for it. The success of the interview will depend to a large degree on what you do beforehand. One essential task is to prepare a list of questions that you will ask during the interview. These questions should be designed to reveal your background and achievements in areas where you know the company is interested.

For example, in your research you may discover that a significant portion of the PE's business involves selling microwave coaxial cable components to the Navy and that the PE has had a great deal of trouble with quality control. If you have a quality control background, write down a question pertaining to this problem that will reveal your expertise in this area. For example: "I understand you have had some reliability problems with your microwave coaxial cable components. Was this an engineering problem or some problem with quality control?" If your background is in marketing, you can ask this leading question: "I understand that you sell microwave coaxial cable components to the Navy. Has marketing been any help in straightening out the quality control problems that you've had?"

Get the PE to talk about his problems. Once you are on the subject, continue to ask intelligent questions. These questions will indicate three things to the PE without your having to say them: (1) you know something important about the PE's company and appreciate his problems; (2) you have experience in areas that the PE is interested in; and (3) you are an expert in these areas.

You should also make a list of questions about the PE's recent successes. If sales have risen markedly over the previous year, ask how the increase was achieved. If the company has made a new acquisition, ask about the general philosophy behind it and whether the company plans to expand. Ask similar questions about declines in sales and divestitures. Formulate a list of questions pertaining to your specialty that you can use in all your interviews. These questions will help to establish your credibility as an expert in your field.

You should use your notes on the PE's executives to help establish rapport, build empathy, relate your background to the interviewing executive, and avoid pitfalls. Look for common interests. Maybe you went to the same school as the hiring executive, were in the same branch of military service, worked for the same company, or worked in the same industry.

If you have something in common, bring it up during the interview: "I hear that you worked for the XYZ Company. I was with them back in 1985." If you are going to be interviewed by the president and discover that you and he have a similar functional background, use this information. Mention it directly if you can, or try to couch your questions and answers in the terms of that specialty. Obviously you should avoid statements that are critical of that specialty.

If you are going to an interview with a company about whose product you know very little, you must spend enough time to acquire at least some specialized knowledge about that product. That is precisely how Allen S. got his job.

Allen had spent the largest part of his career selling radio communications equipment. His interview was with a company developing, manufacturing, and marketing computer peripheral equipment. Allen managed a very successful interview, which ultimately led to a job offer, because in addition to his other qualifications Allen appeared very knowledgeable about the computer peripheral industry. He had spent several hours at his local library boning up on the subject before his interview. Even though Allen said that he had no experience selling computer equipment when he was asked, his questions were to the point and phrased in correct terminology. There was no question in the PE's mind that what Allen didn't know he could learn very rapidly. You must do the same thing Allen did if you are going to an interview with a company that makes a product with which you have had little experience.

● WHAT YOU SHOULD GET FROM YOUR PRE-INTERVIEW RESEARCH

After you finish your pre-interview research, you should have a well thought out list of questions that reveal your general knowledge of the company and its product and your knowledge of your specialty and how it applies to the PE's business. In addition, you should have a list of questions to ask toward the end of your interview if you are fairly certain you have made a sale. These questions are for your protection. Your prospective employer invites you in for an interview to determine if you can do the job. You must determine whether the position meets your job objectives. To do this, you should ask the PE for a detailed description of the position and its specific responsibilities. You should also find out what advanced training is available or required and what growth potential the position has.

At this point, do not ask questions about salary, fringe benefits, health insurance plans, or retirement plans. Defer such questions until you know you will be made a firm offer.

Do not rely on memory or scraps of paper in the interview. Write each question down in a small loose-leaf notebook so you can combine earlier information on a PE with notes you take during the interview. If you use a notebook that fits inside your pocket, you will not need to carry a briefcase.

You will find that most interviewers are other executives, "good guys" who will do everything they can to treat you professionally and put you at ease. However, every so often you will meet an interviewer who believes that putting a job candidate under stress is the most effective way to evaluate him. This type of interview can be sheer torture, but if you are ready for it, you will have an opportunity to look much better than your competition. If fact, you can actually enjoy the process.

● WHAT QUESTIONS YOU MAY BE ASKED AND HOW TO PREPARE FOR THEM

The interviewing environment can generate stress, by the way questions are asked and by the questions themselves. You will not be able to control most factors in the environment. For example, a PE may have several interviewers talk with you simultaneously. The best way to handle this is to speak slowly, listen carefully, and answer only one question at a time. If an interviewer asks a question too rapidly or directly on the heels of someone else's question, ask the interviewer to repeat it. Above all, use the techniques described in this chapter to gain control of the interview.

A few interviewers will really try to get you rattled. They will try such tactics as seating you so that the sun shines directly in your eyes. If this happens, ask politely if you can change your seat to avoid the sun. Never be afraid to tell the interviewer that you are uncomfortable and to explain why. If the heat has been turned up and your interviewer has removed his jacket, ask if the heat can be turned down or if you can remove your jacket as well. Be pleasant and tactful but don't let your interviewer intimidate you.

You cannot do much about the way interviewers ask questions except to ask them to repeat a question if you did not understand it. Never allow yourself to get angry during an interview, regardless of the provocation.

You can do something about questions that cause stress. Prepare yourself for likely stress questions by working out good, solid answers beforehand. Here are some typical stress questions that you should be prepared to answer *before* you go into an interview. Think up some of your own as well.

- Where do you want to be five years from now?
- Where do you think you'll be?
- Are you technical or management oriented? Why?
- Why should we be interested in hiring you?
- What's wrong with your present job?

- Does your present employer know you are out looking for a job?
- Why have you been laid off so many times?
- Why have you made so many job changes?
- Why are you interested in our company?
- Are you ambitious?
- Will you be out to take my job?
- What are your three greatest strengths?
- What are your three greatest weaknesses?
- What do you think of our operation?
- Why do you want to work here?
- Do you feel you have top management potential? Why?
- Are you a good manager?
- Are you a good leader?
- What have you disliked most about past jobs?
- What do you think you would like best about this job?
- If you were just graduating from school and starting your career what would you do differently?
- Are you willing to relocate?
- How important to you is salary versus other aspects of the job?
- What five things have you done in your life (or career) that you are most proud of?
- What does the term "success" mean to you?
- What types of jobs are you looking for?
- If you had your choice of any job at all at this moment, what would that job be and why?
- Why aren't you making more money?
- Where did you stand in your class in college? Why didn't you stand higher?
- Why haven't you accomplished more?
- How have you managed to accomplish so much?

Think through the answers to these questions. Write the answers out and learn them by heart. Then, practice speaking naturally as you give the answers so that you appear to be thinking of your answer as you speak. Practice your interview further with a friend, and ask your friend what you are doing right and what needs polish. Role-playing as practice for an interview can be extremely helpful. If you have a video camera or at least a tape recorder to help you, so much the better. Work at it until you can deliver your answers smoothly and confidently. Before going into any interview, you should be so well prepared that no unusual situation, strange environment, or stress question can shake you or cause you to be ill at ease.

● MENTAL REHEARSAL WILL HELP YOU WIN AT THE INTERVIEW

Psychologist Charles A. Garfield interviewed 1,200 top performers in all fields. One characteristic that clearly set apart top-performing chief executive officers was their ability to mentally rehearse coming actions or events. As reported by *The Wall Street Journal* nearly twenty years ago:

> "Mr. Garfield says he was most surprised by the trait of mental rehearsal, now a popular concept in sports. Top chief executives imagined every facet and feeling of what would have to happen to make a presentation a success, practicing a kind of purposeful daydreaming. A less effective executive, he says, would prepare his facts and agendas but not his psyche."

When I read this article, I realized that I had been practicing mental rehearsal for some years without realizing it. You may have also. The major use I've made of this technique is for speeches. No matter how many times you climb a platform, looking out at your audience can be a bit unnerving. Practicing mental rehearsal lets me get rid of my nervousness during the speech. Also, the mental rehearsal is much faster and can be done at any time or in any place. So, in some ways it is more valuable than a real rehearsal. Since last January, I have recommended mental rehearsal for job interviews, and the feedback I am getting is quite good. I would definitely recommend that you try it.

● ADDITIONAL HINTS FOR MEETING WITH YOUR PE

It goes without saying that you should not be late for an interview. On the other hand, it is unwise to be too early. If you are, you may give your PE the impression that you are too eager for the position. You want the PE to know that you are enthusiastic and interested in the job. You do not want the PE to feel that you are desperate. I recommend that you arrive no more than five minutes early.

Psychologists have discovered that the most critical period of the interview is the first few minutes. It is during this time that the PE decides whether to offer you a job. The remainder of the interview merely reinforces the original decision.

If first impressions really count that much (and they do), then personal appearance is extremely important. Follow these guidelines: Always be well groomed. Dress fashionably, but conservatively. Men should wear a suit and tie. Women should also wear a suit, or a conservative skirt and blouse. Do not wear frayed shirts, old shoes, or any other worn clothing. Do not wear bow ties, mod watches, or sunglasses. A man's chances of being offered a position will be reduced if he has exceptionally long hair, a beard, or a crewcut, unless his PE has the same. I recommend you read *Your Executive Image* by Victoria A. Seitz (Bob Adams Media, Inc., 2000). This book explains the art of self-packaging for both men and women.

Act relaxed, friendly, and enthusiastic. Call the interviewer by name. If you have established a first-name relationship, as covered in the TTP, call your PE by first name. If you have not, introduce yourself thus: "Mr. Smith, I'm Jim Jones. It's good to meet you." State both your first and last name. If the PE gives his or her first name, you may use it during the interview.

Generally it is advantageous to get on a first-name basis with your PE as soon as possible. However, some executive job hunters find this unnatural and uncomfortable. And as mentioned in an earlier chapter, some PEs are more formal. If you feel better about being more formal with the PE, do so. And whether you use first names or not, always treat the PE with respect, but not fear or awe.

In general, it is better not to smoke during the interview. If the interviewer doesn't smoke, she could take offense. If she just quit or is trying to quit, your smoking will not make for a very relaxed meeting. Finally, even if the PE smokes, she could interpret your smoking as a sign of nervousness.

As in any presentation (and an interview is a type of presentation), one key to success is your enthusiasm. You must be enthusiastic. If you are not enthusiastic about yourself, you cannot expect a PE to be very enthusiastic about you.

● HOW TO GAIN CONTROL OF THE INTERVIEW

A basic principle of good interviewing is to get the PE to do most of the talking. Your job is to impress the PE with your brilliance by the quality of your questions, not by a soliloquy of your abilities. To do this, you must capture the initiative subtly, without threatening your PE.

The first moments of the interview will probably be devoted to small talk. You may be asked about how easily you found the PE's office, the weather, your neighborhood, and so forth. If you wish, you can participate in these preliminaries. Comment on something you have in common with the interviewer (maybe you heard that the PE has the same hobby as you), an object in the PE's office, or whatever. This phase of the interview can be very important. You and the PE are sizing each other up. The PE is beginning to form a decision about you, just as you are forming your own attitudes toward the PE.

You must listen carefully for the moment when the preliminaries are over and the serious part of the interview begins. Often, the PE will say something like, "Well, we'd better get on with it," or "Tell me about yourself." You should say something like, "Certainly, but before we start, may I ask you a question?" Stop and wait for the PE to agree. Then ask, "Can you tell me the main qualifications for the job for which I am interviewing?"

As soon as the PE begins to answer, take out your notebook and begin to write. As soon as the PE is finished, go on to the next question and the next. Your objective in using this technique is to impress the PE with your qualifications by the quality of your questions. Also, you want to learn all you can about the job so that when you are asked to describe your experience and accomplishments either during the interview or in a post-interview resume you can tailor them to the requirements of the job.

If for any reason you have not been able to learn beforehand what job the PE has in mind, you should listen especially carefully. At some point the PE will say, "The reason I asked you in is . . . ." If the PE fails to give a reason for inviting you to the interview, try to discover it by saying, "Since you invited me in for this interview, I understand you have need for a _____."

Or you could ask, "Is your need for a _____ due to expansion?" You must get the PE to discuss the reason for the interview so that you can better understand his or her problem. Remember, this is your last chance to get information that will enable you to present your background, accomplishments, and other qualifications as the obvious (but unstated) solution to the PE's problem.

Always avoid giving responses that could disqualify you for the job. Keep the initiative by asking questions and allowing the PE to do most of the talking. But be flexible. Occasionally you will find a PE who is determined to ask the questions. That's fine, but take advantage of every opportunity to demonstrate your knowledge of the company and the interviewing executive or to state experiences that are obviously suited to the PE's needs. If you temporarily lose the initiative because the PE raises a question, answer the question, then recapture the initiative by asking a question of your own. If the PE says, "Tell me about yourself," ask which experience she is most interested in. This will help you in your answer. Here are some other questions you might want to ask:

- Why are you going outside the company to fill this position?
- Whom would I be replacing? Why is that person leaving?
- If I am offered this position and accept it, exactly what will be expected of me?
- What is the number-one priority for the employee who fills this job?

If the interviewer is doing most of the talking, you generally have control and the interview is going well. This does not mean that you sit like a bump on a log responding to questions in monosyllables. It does mean you do less talking because the PE is busy answering your astute and well-thought-out questions.

● HOW TO GAIN INSTANT RAPPORT AND MAINTAIN IT THROUGH THE INTERVIEW

Psychologists discovered some time ago that we act more favorably toward those with whom we are in rapport. The usual way of gaining rapport is finding some commonalty of background, experience, or interest. It's not that you shouldn't try to establish rapport in this way. However, neuro-linguistic programming research demonstrated that there is a faster means. It is called "mirroring."

Mirroring requires matching your PE's voice, speech tempo, word usage, breathing, postures, and movements. You don't mimic in an obvious way. What you do, however, is watch the other person. If they are speaking in a rapid staccato, you start doing the same. If they speak slowly, in a laid back fashion, follow their lead. If they cross a leg, you do the same. Again, don't instantly mimic. Follow the person you are mirroring gradually as you continue with your interview. You're going to have to practice this until it comes naturally and you master it. Once you do, you have an amazing tool for gaining rapport. You will find that you will achieve an almost instant closeness with your PE. It will be as if you have known him or her for years.

Scientists do not know why mirroring works. They do know (and you can verify this for yourself) that people who are already in rapport practice mirroring without any conscious effort. It is as if the brain were saying: "I must like this person, because he is exactly like me."

● HOW TO AVOID SALARY QUESTIONS BEFORE YOU HAVE MADE A SALE

You should not discuss salary until you know that the PE is definitely interested in hiring you. The decision to extend an offer is made fairly early in the interview; compensation is not determined until much later. A figure that may be considered too high or even out of the question early in the interview may be perfectly acceptable after you have "made the sale." Forcing the salary decision too soon may cause the PE to reject you at the start. During the rest of the interview the PE may simply go through the motions, barely listening to what you are saying. Giving a salary figure that is too low can also work against you, since the hiring executive may not consider you "heavy" enough for the job. Once a negative reaction has set in, it is very difficult to overcome.

The only solution is to postpone any discussion of salary until you have made your case and the PE wants to hire you. To do this, you must be prepared to fend off salary questions. If the PE asks what you are currently making or what compensation you are seeking, postpone your answer with one of the following:

- "Like you, I do not have a definite salary figure in mind. However, after we discuss some of the requirements of the job, I'm certain we can arrive at a mutually acceptable figure as to what the job is worth."

- "Salary is, of course, important to me, but it is not the most important factor. I wonder if you could tell me some of the qualifications for the job so I can get a better handle on what the compensation level should be." (This provides an opportunity to lead into your list of questions.)

- "My primary interest is in the total opportunity, rather than in salary alone. If I can ask you a question about the job, I'm certain this will be a great help." (And so does this statement.)

How One of My Graduate Students Got Nearly Twice the Salary He Wanted

One of my former graduate students wrote to tell me this story. We'll call him "Tom." Tom interviewed in a major mid-western city for a job with a large company in the food industry. He had worked out the figures ahead of time, and he calculated that the job he was interviewing for should pay about $50,000 a year, and that met his requirements.

When he met his prospective employer, the very first thing he said was, "Let's cut to the chase. We liked your letter and you've done the kind of things we value. How much do you want?

Taken aback, Tom almost blurted out, "$50,000." However, he remembered what I had taught him. So, he smoothly spoke a line he had practiced, "Look, like you, I don't have a single figure in mind. I investigated your company and you personally, and I liked what I learned about you, too. But if you'll let me defer answering until I understand the job better, I'll be able to give you a much better answer."

His prospective boss paused a moment and then said, "Well, okay, but I want you to know right now, we're not going above $85,000."

Tom was so surprised he could hardly speak. But he managed to mumble that he was pretty certain he could "work it out to $85,000 a year if the job was as good as it sounded."

● HOW TO HANDLE QUESTIONS ABOUT EMPLOYERS AND ACCOMPLISHMENTS

Sometimes a PE will ask questions about your current or former employers. You should never criticize a present or past employer, even if such criticism is well deserved. For one thing, any problem in your past is a negative, even if it was not your fault. Only positive experiences and accomplishments will help you get to job offers. Second, the PE may not agree with your criticism, or you may fail in some way to give all the facts. The net result could be that the PE is silently agreeing with your employer rather than with you. Finally, it may occur to your PE that if you criticize your present or past employer, you may criticize your PE in the future. For similar reasons, you should not betray confidences or competitive information about present or past employers.

If you are asked why you left a former employer or want to leave your present job, you must be ready with an answer. Even if you were or are about to be fired, you should work out an acceptable answer with your former employer. You do not want to give your PE one reason for leaving and have your former employer give another.

In general, you should show your expertise by the quality of your questions and your knowledge of the company, its products, and the PE. If you are asked to describe your experience and accomplishments, state them matter-of-factly and in quantitative terms, as you did in your sales letter. Don't say, "I increased production considerably in a short period of time." Say, "I increased production 50 percent within two months."

● BODY LANGUAGE CAN HELP YOU WIN A JOB

Psychologists have discovered that we frequently reveal our innermost thoughts through visual cues provided by the body. Many salespeople have already begun to use body language in making sales by adjusting their presentation depending on what body language is telling them. You can do the same thing.

Positive Signs

Interviewer is smiling.

Interviewer is leaning forward in the chair.

Interviewer is listening attentively.

Interviewer is nodding affirmatively.

Interviewer's arms are unfolded.

Interviewer is looking directly at you.

Negative Signs

Interviewer is frowning.

Interviewer is drumming fingers on the desk or noticeably playing with some object (such as pen, pencil, or article of clothing).

Interviewer is checking wristwatch periodically.

Interviewer is not making eye contact with you.

Interviewer is squirming around in the seat.

Interviewer's arms are folded across the chest.

If you are getting negative signals, you are doing something wrong. Change tactics and observe what happens.

● WHAT TO DO IF YOU COME UP AGAINST AN EXPERT INTERVIEWER

On rare occasions you will come up against an expert interviewer. Such interviewers will not put you under stress but will do everything possible to put you completely at ease and off guard. They will agree to everything you say and encourage you to say more. They will try to get you to do most of the talking. They will give you the impression that you are continually scoring points during the interview. This is the most dangerous type of interviewer to have. If you are not careful, this interviewer will get you to expose all your weaknesses, which will be coldly evaluated after the interview.

When you encounter the expert interviewer, stay calm and relaxed, but watch what you say and do not lower your guard. Do not allow yourself to be drawn into a discussion of a controversial nature, be it religion, politics, or something closer to the job. No matter how friendly or stimulating your PE, do not discuss beliefs that you know to be held by only a few people and are considered strange by others. Do not state any strong opinions on how your PE should change operations. If you have a unique product that would be a fine addition to your PE's line, don't discuss it until you are hired. Do not exchange any confidences.

Stay away from controversial subjects or causes or even award-winning ideas until you are safely on board with a company. You will have a much better idea of what your new company can do and what ideas can be politically sold. Your task at this time is to sell one product: yourself. Do not make it twice as difficult by trying to sell something else at the same time.

Remember, everything you say to a PE will either boost or lower your chances of receiving a job offer. Stick to information that you know will boost your chances.

How Boyd T. Lost a Job Offer
Because of a Pet Belief

Boyd T.'s interview went quite well until he discovered that both he and the PE were avid readers of science fiction. This common interest should have built empathy with the PE. However, Boyd had a pet belief that is generally considered a bit eccentric, even though many famous people share it. Boyd believed that the earth was being visited by beings from another galaxy. Boyd went into some depth on this topic, and the PE appeared both interested and enthusiastic. He encouraged Boyd to go on. Boyd did. By the end of the interview Boyd felt that he "had it made." His PE had been most friendly and agreeable. Boyd never heard from the PE again.

What went wrong? True, the hiring executive was a science fiction buff; he even thought that extraterrestrial surveillance was an interesting topic and that Boyd's arguments had merit. But the PE's company was a very conservative one, and interest in science fiction was limited to the individual who interviewed Boyd. The interviewer knew that if he hired Boyd, Boyd would be dealing on a daily basis with people who not only didn't read science fiction but would think of anyone with Boyd's beliefs was a crackpot. He reasoned that if Boyd could expose such private beliefs to a complete stranger, what might he say to his associates after joining the company? Even though the PE had a great deal of empathy with Boyd, he decided not to extend an offer.

How Joe B. Lost a Job Because of a Good Idea

Joe B. was interviewing smoothly. Suddenly, he saw the answer to a problem his PE mentioned. It was a product that would fit exactly into his PE's product line. Moreover, this was Joe's pet project, one he had almost finished years previously. He launched into the presentation of a detailed business plan. What Joe didn't know was that someone else in the PE's company had the same idea previously. It had turned into a political battle that the interviewer himself had barely survived. In fact, the interviewer to whom Joe so enthusiastically explained his plan was the very one who was instrumental in killing the idea. Although in many ways Joe was the ideal candidate, he didn't get an offer either.

● HOW TO GAUGE THE PROGRESS OF THE INTERVIEW

Sometimes you will get the impression that the interview is not going well and that you are going to be rejected. Conceal your feelings and continue with the interview as if nothing had happened. It may be only the personality or mood of your interviewer. Perhaps he had a bad day or has other things on his mind. Keep your enthusiasm and positive mental attitude throughout the interview.

How can you tell whether the interview is going well? There are three definite signs, in addition to the body language cues mentioned earlier:

* the interviewer does more talking than you;
* the interviewer brings up salary or fringe benefits toward the end of the interview; and
* the interviewer speaks of bringing you in again to meet other members of his staff.

● HOW TO CLOSE OUT THE INTERVIEW WITH A SALE

Never leave matters hanging at the end of the interview. If you are interested in the position, let your interviewer know it. Say something like, "I am very interested in this position. Can I expect to hear from you by Monday or Wednesday?" Or say, "The job definitely interests me. What is our next step?"

If the PE makes you an offer on the spot, do not accept immediately. Tell the PE that you are definitely interested but would like a few days to think it over. Do not say that you want to discuss it with your family, even if you do. Many PEs like to maintain the illusion that their employees are independent of their families in matters related to their careers.

If your interviewer is vague about making you an offer or about taking further action, you must regain control of the situation. Tell your PE something like this: "I want to be completely frank with you. You have a very fine company here, and I consider the position we have spoken about to be an excellent opportunity for me to do an outstanding job. However, I have another offer pending, and I must respond within the week. When will you be making me an offer?"

If you feel that you have definitely made a sale, it is time to make your salary requirements known. The PE may raise this question himself. You should be ready to use the techniques described in Chapter 19 to negotiate the highest salary that you can. If you bring up the subject yourself, combine your requirements with other remarks. Tell your PE that you have another offer pending at $X and therefore would like to receive his offer as soon as possible.

The PE may delay extending you an offer because she is not fully sold on hiring you and wants to interview other candidates. If you allow the PE this chance, you could very well lose the job offer. Always remember that you are in a competitive situation. Go after and get the offer, even if you are not completely sold on the job yourself. You should be the one with several options, not your PE.

To have several offers to consider, you must aggressively go after the offer at every interview. Be smooth, polished, and dignified, but keep the pressure on your PE. Let him or her know that you have other offers pending.

● DEFINITE DO'S

1. Be on time for the interview.
2. Dress fashionably but conservatively.
3. Be well groomed.
4. Be relaxed, enthusiastic, and friendly.
5. Be self-confident.
6. Call the interviewer by name.
7. Shake hands firmly.
8. Maintain eye contact.
9. Be a good listener.
10. Sell yourself indirectly and subtly.
11. Take notes.
12. Describe your accomplishments in quantitative terms.
13. Protect the confidence of your present or past employers.

14. If asked about your health, state that your health is excellent and do not discuss private medical problems.

15. Answer questions directly and without hesitation.

16. Get the full name and title of the executive who interviews you.

17. Prepare well and completely before the interview.

● **DEFINITE DON'TS**

1. Wear frayed shirts, old clothes, bow ties, mod watches, or sunglasses inside a building.

2. Smoke.

3. Chew gum.

4. Be reticent about answering questions on your experience and accomplishments.

5. Be overly aggressive or arrogant.

6. Criticize your present or past employers.

7. Apologize for any shortcomings.

8. Appear to pose a threat to your potential supervisor's position.

9. Read the mail on your interviewer's desk.

10. Look at your watch, drum your fingers, or in any other way show nervousness, boredom, or impatience.

11. Argue or allow yourself to be drawn into a discussion of controversial subjects.

12. State or imply that you can work miracles.

13. Bring in unsolicited examples of your work.

14. Inquire about salary, vacation, or other fringe benefits until you are definite that the PE is interested in hiring you.

The Main Point

Like everything else in life, those who are great interviewees become so by learning what they must do and practicing these techniques to perfection. You can do the same.

**SUPPLY REFERENCES
WHEN ASKED**

13

HOW TO REFUSE TO SUPPLY REFERENCES AND HAVE SUPERIOR REFERENCE CHECKS

"My voice shook a little when I told her I'd give her the names and address on 'mutual interest.' At first she didn't know what I meant. She even called her supervisor. Then, she saw what I had written and just smiled and said it was okay."

—A Recent Job Candidate

// "You mean I'm not supposed to give the PE my references, even when asked?" I know you are probably thinking that this time I really "flipped out." Most job seekers feel that being asked for references is a really good sign, a sign of interest by your PE. They cannot imagine why references shouldn't be eagerly put forward. Believe me, there are very real reasons why you must break this rule and not supply references when asked.

● WHY YOU SHOULD NOT SUPPLY REFERENCES EVEN WHEN REQUESTED DIRECTLY BY YOUR PE

You may think that when your PE asks for references he is on the verge of making you a job offer. Usually this is not the case. Most HR departments of large, and many smaller companies ask all applicants for references on a routine basis. Some even demand references in their advertisements for jobs. Moreover, if the HR staff is large and they have the time, they may routinely call all references even if the chance of your being invited to an interview is slim.

Now when they do this, here's what happens. If your reference is a good one, and we will assume that it is, although later I will show you that this may not be so, you get a good reference. If you have prepared your reference as you should, it is not only a good reference, your reference is enthusiastic. All well and good. But, if you have followed my advice, you want to end up with five or more job offers maturing at the same time. So you have talked to many potential PE's and have responded to a good number job advertisements. If you keep on giving out your references, your reference is going to get called again. Well and good. Once again, your reference, properly prepared, will enthusiastically give you a good reference. But what if he or she is called a third time, or a fourth. I once heard of a single reference who was called ten times. As this man told me, "Along about call number six or seven, I wasn't quite as enthusiastic."

Moreover, supplying references shouldn't be a square-filler. This is a chance for you to look much stronger than your competition. So, you shouldn't pick friends or relatives, or just anyone as references unless they are prominent or hold positions of importance. To make my point by a little exaggeration, if you are a PE would you be more impressed calling a former President of the United States as a reference for someone you want to hire, or someone's Aunt Milly or high school chum? The only problem is your Aunt Milly or high school friend probably has a lot more time than someone of some importance does. You can't afford to jeopardize a really great reference. So, don't give it . . . at least not until the final stages when you know that the reference check is the final step between you and the job offer.

● HOW TO AVOID GIVING YOUR REFERENCES PREMATURELY AND HAVE THEM LOVE YOU FOR IT

It is fairly easy to avoid having to give references early in the process with any particular PE. If you are currently employed, you can plead sensitivity to being discovered looking for a job elsewhere and promise to provide references at a later date. Most PEs will accept this.

If they don't, or if you are sent one of those monster personnel forms to complete right at the start, you have an opportunity to gain a competitive advantage even while refusing to give them the information they want.

First, you don't want to waste your time completing one of those monster job applicant forms out anyway unless there is a specific job you are being considered for. Usually it is HR that sends you one of these. Your prospective boss won't. So ask the HR representative what job you are being considered for. If he or she can't tell you a specific job, my advice is not to waste your time.

A large corporation may attempt to trap you into completing one of these forms by scheduling you to drop by the company's HR a half hour or so prior to your interview with the PE, even if you have gained an interview with him on your own. You arrive at HR and they present you with a table and chair and one of these monster personnel forms to fill out. If you do it, it will document not your references but your compensation history. It will put you at a tremendous negotiating disadvantage even if you get the offer.

Before we get to how to handle the references, this is as good a place as any to tell you how to avoid spilling your guts for later negotiations. When asked for salary history, I always tell the HR interviewer that I don't remember the exact amount I was making and offer to send it in later when I can check it out. Usually they won't let you get away with that. Remember they aren't working for *you*. They want to make sure they have all the information to get you at the lowest price they can. So likely as not, they will tell you to estimate the salary. Great. I put a little note on the form indicating I have been instructed to estimate my salary history since I don't have accurate figures with me. I then "estimate" a salary history which will not put me at a disadvantage should we enter salary negotiations.

Let's get back to references. I said that references should be an opportunity. You can make it so by picking the most important-sounding people you know as references. If you know a company president, he or she is a great reference. If you have a former professor who liked you and who is well-known or is a book author, that's a great reference. If you sit on any boards of directors you probably know dozens of prominent people or people in positions that others will recognize. Pick your references carefully. Once you have five important people who have agreed to be references for you, you are ready to go. Write out their titles only: "An internationally known professor of finance." "The president of an important company in our geographical location." "A former U.S. Senator." "The CEO of an international corporation." "A former president of the Screen Actors Guild." "A winner of a national award for the best advertising campaign of the year." "A best-selling business book author." Such titles are only limited by your contacts, their willingness to serve as a reference for you, and their relevance to the position you are interested in. Obviously, the more relevant to your future job, the better.

List each title, one for each reference required. Then put, "names, addresses, and phone numbers of these important people who have agreed to be my reference will be furnished on mutual interest."

I like that term, "mutual interest." It means such time as you are offered a job and you are interested enough to accept. That's mutual interest. It takes you out of the realm of supplicant and puts you more on a equal footing with those who would hire you.

● WHY COMPANIES MAKE REFERENCE CHECKS

Most companies use reference checks as one means of verifying your background. You can expect complete checks once there is "mutual interest" and a job offer is extended, or at least after you have become a serious candidate for the job. Frequently checks are made not only on those people you supply as references (the PE assumes that these will be good, or why would you have given them?) but also on former supervisors, associates, and even subordinates. Keep in mind that the PE can contact anyone who may be able to comment on your work experience, character, or ability. Sometimes an offer is made contingent on your references "checking out." In this case, the reference check is the final hurdle. It can eliminate otherwise well-qualified candidates or cause them to lose out to competitors with better references.

More frequently than you might think, job hunters get poor recommendations from supposedly excellent references. Executive recruiters discover this all the time in checking references supplied by their candidates. Here are examples from the files of headhunters.

How Don G. Got a Bad Reference from
His Former College Roommate

Don G., a brilliant young physicist, received his PhD with honors and spent eight years with one firm. He gained an excellent professional reputation and was promoted well ahead of his contemporaries. When a headhunter for a position as manager of research and development recruited Don, he listed his roommate from his graduate days in college as a personal reference.

All Don's references checked out; in fact, they were outstanding. That is, all but one. Don's former roommate said the following: "Don is a nice fellow, but not very reliable. I guess you know it took him five years to get his bachelor's degree. Also, I've heard that he was moved up too fast in his present company, and I'm certain that's going to block any future promotions for him. I guess he'd be okay as a manager as long as he were closely supervised."

How Mort T. Got a Bad Reference After
Saving His Company

Mort T. was a general manager who saved several companies from bankruptcy and made them profitable. He was acclaimed in his field by customers, competitors, and associates alike. In his next-to-last job, as president reporting to a chief executive officer, he had pulled a company out of the red, more than doubled sales, and built more organizational elan than any manager before or since. Here's what Mort's former boss said when contacted by a headhunter: "Mort was an outstanding leader, but he was very stubborn and would never take advice. He did a good to excellent job but couldn't seem to get along with anyone. I really can't recommend him."

Because of this unexpected response, the headhunter called other executives at the company to ask about Mort. The first corporate officer at Mort's level said, "Mort is a superior manager, a very gifted guy who turned the company around." The financial executive at Mort's old company commented, "Mort really knows his stuff. He has the knack of knowing exactly what to do to get everyone pulling in the same direction." Finally, Mort's replacement, his former deputy, told the headhunter, "A very hard act to follow. Mort did things for this company that I don't think anyone else could have done. He had everybody working overtime and actually loving it."

● WHY JOB HUNTERS ARE GIVEN BAD REFERENCES

There are dozens of stories of executives whose references did not check out, although by logic and reason they should have. Can you imagine what might have happened had any of the above references been the only one who could be reached? Or what if the job hunter was really unlucky and two of his references failed to check out? What would be the results if the competition between two job candidates was particularly close?

Why are job hunters like Don and Mort given unfair references? The motivation can be jealousy. Don's former roommate was also a physicist. Don had forged ahead and was ready to take over major responsibilities as an R&D manager. Don's friend was still at square one. Mort's former supervisor resented Mort's accomplishments and saw him as a threat to his own position. In fact he was half-afraid that the headhunter was recruiting Mort for his very job. Mort's superior performance made it impossible for the corporate officer to fire him, but this did not prevent him from giving Mort a bad reference.

● THE SECRET OF ALWAYS GIVING SUPERIOR REFERENCES

What can you do to prevent your references from unexpectedly turning sour? First, prepare your references before they are contacted. If you are not conducting a campaign in secret, talk to each potential reference, including former employers. Tell each your job objective and explain what you would like the reference to say. Don't be bashful. If you did a great job for some people and you'd like them to emphasize it, tell them. This preparation is especially important with a former employer, since you must establish an agreed-on and acceptable reason for leaving your job.

Second, try to locate any hidden bombs before they go off. Have every reference checked out. If there is any doubt about a reference, one way to do this is to have a friend check them for you. Make up a list of at least ten questions that a PE or headhunter might ask: "Under what circumstances do you know the candidate?" "What kind of person is she?" "Is he reliable?" "Is he suited to management?" Review these questions with your reference checker and make certain that he sounds professional. Your checker's dialogue might go something like this: "Hello, Mrs. Smith? This is Clark Baker of Worldwide Search. One of your former employees, Jim Jones, is being considered for a senior financial position with one of my clients. I wonder if I could take a few minutes of your time for a reference check?"

No matter what happens, your checker must not admit that he is anything except what he says he is. If he is asked questions about the job, company, or industry, he should say that he is not permitted to divulge this information.

If you discover a bad reference, don't use it. If the reference is a personal or professional one, just substitute a good reference. What can you do if the reference is a former supervisor? Well, if you don't name the former company, your former supervisor won't be contacted. If the PE insists that you name former companies, you can give the names and numbers of good references at each company and leave out your former supervisor. If you locate only one bad reference among former supervisors, try to find out the reason for it. Tell your PE about it and offer him good references at the same company.

● WHAT TO DO AFTER YOUR REFERENCES HAVE BEEN VERIFIED

Once you have completed your checking, make a list of dependable personal, professional, and former employer references. Always make sure that these references are not called until you are definitely interested in a job offered by a PE and the PE is definitely interested in you. If you do not protect your references, along about check number ten your references are going to become somewhat less than enthusiastic about you. Protect your references by adopting the policy that "references will be furnished only if there is mutual interest." If your references are senior, give your PE a hint by listing titles only as indicated previously.

The Main Point

The reference check is one of the final obstacles between you and a great job. Prepare for it properly and it is a competitive advantage even though you don't furnish your references on demand. Fail to give the references the attention you should, and it can cost you a great job.

**PSYCHOLOGICAL TESTS—
JUST DO WHAT THEY SAY**

14

HOW TO BEAT PSYCHOLOGICAL TESTS

"The first time someone gave me the stupid test, they told me I wasn't right for the job. I learned later from a friend who is a psychologist that they had really misused this test. He told me how I should answer the questions if I took it again. I did and got hired. That was ten years and three promotions ago."

—A Senior Plant Manager

Psychological tests are designed to evaluate your capabilities and limitations—in short, your strengths and weaknesses. They measure, or attempt to measure, almost anything from intelligence, to sanity, to manual and mental dexterity.

Psychological testing came into wide use after World War II, reaching a peak in the late 1950s and early 1960s. There is periodic resurgence in their use, and some companies give such tests today. Handling this particular hurdle can be just as important as other challenges you meet in your job campaign.

● WHY YOU SHOULD BE WARY OF PSYCHOLOGICAL TESTS

Are psychological tests accurate? Well, they *can* be. If this is true, why not go in straight and unprepared and let the chips fall where they may? For one thing, some PEs do not use tests properly. Even though they have had little training in administering tests or interpreting their results, they attempt to do both.

One sales firm gave all its job candidates a test and required a minimum score before extending an offer. High scorers were given preference over low scorers, regardless of a candidate's accomplishments. After several years the personnel manager became suspicious because of the turnover in sales personnel in the company. An independent consultant was hired. His analysis showed that for this company's type of selling, scores above the minimum set by the firm were excellent predictors of failure, not success. Because of the tests, the company had consistently rejected candidates who were likely to succeed.

Another reason to be wary of psychological tests is that some PEs may set unrealistically high scoring requirements. In one state the Board of Education required candidates for high school teaching positions to score in the upper 2 percent of an IQ test. Now there are only a limited number of people in this IQ group; they are not all high school teachers and not all congregate in one state. Yet this state's school system had no trouble finding qualified teachers. How was this possible? You guessed it. Those candidates who wanted the job badly enough prepared for the test, took practice exams, and spent time working on their weak areas until they could score at the required level.

Some firms that use psychological testing in hiring give so much weight to the tests that the hiring decision is determined almost solely by the test results. But according to Dr. Irwin Rodman, a psychologist whose practice includes testing for major firms, any testing professional who is allowed to make decisions about a candidate's suitability for employment is "Whistling Dixie." Dr. Rodman was quoted in the May 1982 issue of *American Business* as saying, "He's not an accountant or an engineer. He's a psychologist and he has to make clear to his corporate clientele that his technical expertise and only his expertise—is what's involved." Psychological factors should never be the most important consideration in a hiring decision. But many firms have a childlike faith in these tests—they make them the most important consideration.

Probably the best predictive test ever developed was one used to measure success in aircrew training during World War II. Almost 200,000 aviators or would-be aviators took this test, so the size of the sample population was significant. A descendant of the original test is still used today. How successful was this most successful of tests? It had a validity coefficient of .64. (A "perfect" test would have a validity coefficient of 1.0.) If you think that this doesn't sound very high, read on.

If those candidates who failed the aircraft test had been admitted into training anyway, statistics show that 56 percent would still have passed the course. Why weren't they admitted? It wasn't cost-effective to have 44 percent of a class of pilots flunk out. Further, even this most successful of tests was predicting success in *training*. It said nothing about success in combat. Most tests have a much lower validity coefficient than the one for aircrew selection. In fact, for the complicated skills of managers and many professionals, the correlation between test scores and performance is usually less than .50.

Some people are poor test takers. For whatever reason, they consistently score lower than other executives whom they easily outperform on the job. If you have a good background and skills that are in reasonable demand, but you know that you fall short of being the world's finest test taker, your best tactic may be not to take a test at all. Tell your PE that, with your accomplishments, you do not feel you should be required to take a test. If there is any doubt at all, you would be happy to furnish references to verify the information you have provided. If the PE is really interested, you will probably not be required to take a test.

● HOW TO PREPARE FOR PSYCHOLOGICAL TESTING

Preparation for any type of psychological test takes time—time you could more profitably use to get interviews. Therefore, do not go into lengthy preparations for psychological testing until you know you are going to be tested and can get some insight into what kind of test you may be given.

To prepare for psychological testing, I recommend that you take general tests offered by a university psychology department or by firms specializing in psychological testing. The latter source can be quite expensive, so if you have already had experience with such tests and have an idea how well you do, skip this phase.

If you have the chance, you should read books on psychological testing. I recommend *Psychological Testing,* by Anne Anastasi and Susana Urbina (Prentice Hall); *Psychological Testing: Study Guide* by Susana Urbina (Prentice Hall); *The Brain Watchers,* by Martin L. Gross (Random House); and *Theory and Practice of Psychological Testing,* by Frank S. Freeman (Holt, Rinehart and Winston). In addition, *The Organization Man,* by William H. Whyte, Jr. (Simon & Schuster), has two useful chapters: "How Good an Organization Man Are You?" and "The Tests of Conformity." It also has a valuable appendix entitled "How to Cheat on Personality Tests."

● HOW TO GET COPIES OF SAMPLE TESTS

Copies of the following sample intelligence, personality, and interest tests are available from several sources:

Typical Intelligence Tests

Stanford-Binet, Wechsler Adult Intelligence Scale, Wonderlic Personnel Test, Otis Employment Test, Wesman Personnel Classification Test

Typical Personality Tests

California Psychological Inventory, Minnesota Multiphasic Personality Inventory, Personal Orientation Inventory, Thurstone Temperament Scale

Typical Interest (Vocational) Tests

Minnesota Vocational Interest Inventory, Strong Vocational Interest Blank, Occupational Interest Inventory, Kuder Occupational Interest Survey

You can obtain sample tests from friends in large personnel departments, psychological testing firms, or universities. Or you can write to companies that publish psychological tests and ask for their catalogs. Here are a few:

- American Guidance Service, Inc., Publishers' Building, Circle Pines, Minnesota 55014

- California Test Bureau, Del Monte Research Park, Monterey, California 93940
- Center for Applications of Psychological Type, 2815 NW 13th St., Suite 401, Gainesville, Florida 32609
- Consulting Psychologists Press, Inc., 3803 Bayshore Road, Palo Alto, California 94303
- Educational and Industrial Testing Service, P.O. Box 7234, San Diego, California 92107
- Houghton Mifflin Company, 1 Beacon Street, Boston, Massachusetts 02107
- Psychological Corporation, 757 Third Avenue, New York, N.Y. 10017
- Science Research Associates, Inc., 259 East Erie Street, Chicago, Illinois 60611
- E. F. Wonderlic and Associates, P.O. Box 7, Northfield, Illinois 60094

Don't spend a lot of time preparing for psychological tests until you know you have to take them. Then, concentrate on the type of test you will be given and the areas in which you need to improve. For example, intelligence tests are generally divided into quantitative and verbal parts. If you are weak on the verbal side, concentrate on your vocabulary and reading ability. If you are weak on quantitative problems, concentrate on basic math, algebra, trigonometry, and geometry. The Graduate Record Examination (GRE), used by many colleges and universities, is a good general intelligence test. *How to Pass the Graduate Record Examination,* by David R. Turner (ARCO), is full of practice tests. You can find other manuals like this at college and university bookstores.

● TWO GENERAL RULES FOR PASSING TESTS

There are two general rules on how to "pass" psychological tests. First, answer personality tests as if you were an average, middle-class person in your profession. Respond the way you think this average person would answer, not you. Don't favor any strange or radical views. Second, answer interest tests in a way that someone vitally interested in a career field would answer. That is, if you take two interest tests for a teaching position, one at College A for an English professor and the other at College B for an athletic director, your interest scales should reflect more introspective, scholarly concerns for College A and outdoorsy, leadership-type action teaching for College B.

If you are going to lie on a test, make certain that you do so consistently. Many personality and interest tests have liar scales that document your success or failure in trying to influence. These scales are based on a lack of consistency in answering the same question presented in several different ways. For example, the following true-false questions might be scattered throughout a single test:

- I prefer indoor activities, such as reading, to outdoor activities, such as sports.
- I spend most of my free time outdoors.
- I would prefer swimming, fishing, and walking over reading, playing chess, or listening to music.
- I would prefer boating, mountain climbing, or sunbathing over collecting stamps, doing crossword puzzles, or painting.
- My hobbies are mostly indoor activities.

A failure to answer all these questions to show a preference for either indoor or outdoor activities would affect your overall score on the liar's scale. If you answer enough sets of questions inconsistently, your score on that particular scale will suffer, as will your credibility on that particular test.

The Main Point

Many companies that use psychological tests misuse them, and the results may be meaningless anyway. If a company insists on giving you a psychological test as a condition for employment, don't despair. You can beat such tests successfully.

AFTER THE INTERVIEW, SEND A LETTER THANKING YOUR PROSPECTIVE EMPLOYER FOR THE INTERVIEW

15

WHAT YOU SHOULD DO AFTER THE INTERVIEW TO GREATLY INCREASE YOUR CHANCES OF GETTING AN OFFER

"When I applied to the holding company out of state, I didn't think I had a chance because it wasn't my emphasis in the MBA program. I was even less confident when the vice president told me they were interviewing the ten best candidates and only hiring one. I mean, I didn't even go to a 'ranked' business school. I was very surprised when I was asked to be one of those ten. I thought the interview went well. I was very tempted to send one of those nice thank you notes. I didn't. However, I did get the job. Thanks again."

—A Recent MBA Graduate

veryone says "Send a thank you letter after the interview." If you are really able to benefit your PE so much, what are you thanking the PE for? You gave him or her the opportunity of seeing what remarkable things you could be doing for your PE's company. You gave up your time in order to do so. If you are what you claim to be, the PE should be thanking you. I know that sounds arrogant. I want to be intentionally arrogant here to make the point. You don't owe the PE anything for the interview. And if you are writing just to "suck up," that's despicable.

● WHAT YOU SHOULD DO IMMEDIATELY AFTER THE INTERVIEW

When you return home after the interview, take out your notes and go over them. Combine them with your pre-interview notes so that you have a complete picture of your PE, the job, and the company. Fill in additional information that you think is pertinent. Do this as soon as possible after the interview, while you still have the facts in mind. You will be surprised several days later at just how little you remember. This is especially true if you have one or two additional interviews in the interim. Also, many hiring decisions are made soon after the interview, so it is to your advantage to get this additional material to the PE as quickly as possible before the final decision is made. You present these facts in a follow-up sales letter.

● THE FOLLOW-UP SALES LETTER

The purpose of the follow-up sales letter is to remind your PE of how your experience and accomplishments are suited to his or her needs. You should send the letter only if you did not receive a job offer during the interview. You can include a special resume if the PE has requested one. At this point, because you know the position and understand what the PE is looking for, you can tailor your qualifications so that they make sense to your PE in the context of this particular job.

The interview follow-up sales letter will assist you in getting the best job offer. It will convince undecided PEs that they should hire you by providing additional, documented support of your qualifications and reinforcing information you have previously given during the interview. It will also help you win out over your competitors by showing that you are the one individual who has the right experience and capabilities for the job.

Dear George;

Since our meeting this morning, I have had an opportunity to review the notes I made, the requirements of the job, and my own capabilities and accomplishments. Seeing these laid out before me confirms what I previously felt: that I can make a very smooth transition and rapid contribution to your operations in the capacity of vice president and general manager of your instrument and controls division.

It appears to me that the division's previous year's financial loss is not catastrophic and that the situation can be turned around during this fiscal year. As you indicated, you have already initiated corrective action in bidding procedures to prevent a reoccurrence of excessively low bidding. Aside from these problems, the company and current market conditions offer a number of opportunities for expansion and increased profits. It is certainly comparable to the challenge I met when I took H&R Engineering from a $5 million loss to a $40 million profit in one year a few years ago.

You have indicated that this division needs a forceful leader with an extensive technical background in engineering and project management of government contracts.

I am probably unique in my qualifications for this role. As program manager in NASA, I you will recall that I directed three successful programs in excess of $10 million, each of which came in early and under budget. Recruited into industry, I held every position from program manager through R&D director and division general manager. In total, I managed $300 million in government contracts over a five-year period.

The position of general manager is a senior one and will require considerable interaction with senior government personnel. Therefore, as you explained, the job requires not only high-level technical experience but also senior contacts in government. My contacts include 19 military officers of general or admiral rank and 25 civilian employees who are in the Senior Executive Service. I consider all of these individuals friends, and all will take my telephone calls and would be willing to listen to my ideas.

Because of the peculiar nature of government business, your new general manager must have extensive experience in preparing and bidding on responses to IFBs, RFPs, and RFQs, as well as a sound grounding in bid/no bid decision making. I have bid on government contracts and while in government, evaluated 52 such bids. I led the government team that evaluated the propulsion subsystem of the Sea Dragon Missile and five lessor efforts. This experience assisted me a good deal in industry. I believe this learning experience was a major factor in winning nine of ten major programs that were bid under my direction. My batting average for programs over $100,000 is 82%.

George, I enjoyed meeting with you and am very interested in the job. I look forward to hearing from you, and hopefully working for you.

Sincerely,

Figure 15.1. Sample interview follow-up letter.

● HOW TO WRITE THE FOLLOW-UP SALES LETTER

The follow-up sales letter is constructed much like a response to an advertisement. Use the notes you made during the interview to define the requirements of the job. Go over each requirement or need stated by your PE during the interview. Show how qualified you are for each one by documenting what you have accomplished in each area. Don't forget to quantify each accomplishment, just as you did in writing the sales letter or in preparing a response to an advertisement. You may vary the format if you wish to refer to something that you discussed with the PE. Keep the letter informal and don't make it appear too much like a resume.

Figure 15.1 is a sample interview follow-up letter. There is no way the writer could have prepared such a letter before the interview. The writer considered himself primarily a marketer. He had extensive marketing management experience and even an MBA in marketing. However, he also has high-level engineering management experience and high level experience in government. In the follow-up sales letter he emphasizes his engineering experience because during the interview he discovered that his PE saw the job primarily as a general management position that required a heavy technical management background. In fact, the PE felt that the job did not require any functional experience in marketing at all. So, he down-played his marketing background and emphasized other aspects that his PE felt were important.

In addition, he restated each job requirement mentioned by the PE during the interview. Restating the job requirements you learned during the interview shows the PE that you understand his problems and confirms your ability to meet his requirements. Your interview follow-up sales letter will set you apart from other candidates seeking the job and will increase your ratio of offers to interviews. It is a must if you are serious about getting a great job.

The Main Point

If you want a great job fast, don't send out a thank you letter after the interview. Instead, send out an immediate follow-up sales letter.

**WHEN YOU GET AN
OFFER, ACCEPT IT
RIGHT AWAY**

16

HOW TO DELAY ACCEPTANCE AND NEGOTIATE A HIGHER SALARY

"I graduated from an average law school, with average grades, but an intense desire to obtain for myself an above-average salary at a prestigious law firm. As a result of employing your strategies, I am employed at a major downtown law firm, engaged in business litigation. I am paid a salary fully commensurate with my expectations. Further, I find it a continual source of pleasure and amusement in knowing that two of my law school classmates, both finishing in the top 5% of our class are also at my firm. But they receive a salary $5000 less than I receive."

—An Attorney at a Los Angeles Law Firm

The "experts" tell us that when you get an offer, this is the end of the process. All you need to do is accept it. This rule is 100% wrong. When you get an offer, this is the start of a very important part of the job-finding process. It is called the negotiation phase, and you skip it at your own peril.

● IF THERE IS ANY "RULE," IT IS THAT YOU MUST NEGOTIATE

Whether you really want the biggest salary you can get or not, and most of us want exactly that, you must always negotiate your salary. Never automatically accept what is offered. Otherwise, your PE will feel cheated. He or she will suspect that more was paid for you than was necessary. You will have devalued yourself for your new job right at the start. So, no matter how uncomfortable you are with negotiating, no matter how much you would prefer just to accept the offer and be done with it, no matter even if the offer is higher than you expected, you must negotiate. When does negotiation start? Earlier than you may think.

● THE PRE-NEGOTIATION STAGE

The Pre-negotiation stage is the period before you have made the sale of yourself, before your prospective boss has decided to hire you. Up to this point, if you have done what I recommended, you have deferred all talk of compensation. However, everything you do is really part of your salary negotiation, from the quality of your sales letters to the way you speak on the phone, to how you dress and how you present yourself. And remember, if your interviewer wants to talk about salary before you have made a sale, use the techniques covered in Chapter 10.

At some point, however, you must focus on salary negotiation. Sometimes this is during the first interview. Sometimes this may occur at a later interview, or even over the phone. Let's look at negotiation during the initial interview.

● NEGOTIATION DURING THE INITIAL INTERVIEW

Perhaps the interview has been going well. You can see where things are headed. It is time to begin. Your objective is to give salary guidance to your PE while avoiding direct questions or discussions of salary. You want to make an indirect approach.

The best approach is always an indirect one. This allows you to sense the size of the offer before it is made, and also allows you to give clues to your negotiating partner. For example, one way you might do this is to describe an experience you had with your company car in a former company. This will alert the PE to the fact that you expect a company car or equivalent compensation. Or you can tell a story about a subordinate and mention his salary. The salary level you assign to your subordinate will give the PE an idea of what salary you expect. Say anything you want in the way of a subtle hint, but do not state your compensation requirements explicitly. Again, these are part of pre-negotiations. You are not yet in actual negotiations.

● HOW DO YOU KNOW WHEN ACTUAL NEGOTIATIONS BEGIN?

The key to success in the interview, or in any dialogue with the PE, is to listen. By listening carefully you will know when you are about to get an offer. The PE will begin to sell the job to you. He or she will describe the advantages of the job, the company, working conditions, or recreational opportunities. The crucial moment is when the PE begins to describe fringe benefits. This is one reason that you should not bring up fringe benefits yourself. If you allow your PE to do it, you will know that you have made a sale and will gain a psychological advantage in negotiation.

● HOW TO AVOID NEGOTIATING FROM YOUR OLD SALARY

In many human endeavors there are guiding principles of success that must be observed. In salary negotiations there is such a principle. It can be stated simply: *If you are trying to negotiate a significant increase in salary, do not make your present or previous salary the basis of negotiations.*

If you are already making a satisfactory salary, you may be seeking a great job for another reason. Maybe you want to improve your opportunity for advancement. Or, perhaps you want to get out of an impossible political situation in your old company, or get away from a dysfunctional boss. In these cases, you may want to reveal your previous salary and negotiate from there.

If you are after a significant salary increase, there is an important fact that you must know. Most companies will try to use your previous salary as a starting point for negotiations and will try to limit increases to 10 to 15 percent of your previous salary. Yes, even though this policy is obviously shortsighted, the average PE wants to get a bargain. A bargain to him is as close to your previous salary as possible, assuming your previous salary is not high and he has no other guidelines.

To avoid negotiating from your old salary, you must give your PE some other basis for negotiations. The real basis is what you are worth to that company, and to this company's competitors. Also, you want to get a good idea of exactly what you are worth so you do not inadvertently price yourself out of the market and so you can speak with authority when discussing salary with a PE. Prepare your research carefully before you begin overt negotiations. Before going into the interview, you should obtain accurate salary information about the job, taking into account industry, function, job title, geographical location, and size of company. You can obtain this information from a variety of sources. Use as many as possible so that you can cross check information.

Some general reference books are available. These include:

- *The American Almanac of Jobs and Salaries* by John Wright (Avon Books)
- American Salaries and Wages Survey: Statistical Data Derived from More Than 300 Government, Business & News Sources (5th Ed) by *Helen S. Fisher (The Gale Group)*
- *Occupational Outlook Handbook* (U.S. Department of Labor)

The internet also has sources of salary information. Here are a few sites to check out:

- http://www.espan.com
- http://www.jobstar.org
- http://www.erieri.com
- http://www.acinet.org
- http://www.careerbabe.com
- http://www.wageweb.com
- http://www.pencomsi.com
- http://www.realrates.com

Other sources of salary information include professional and trade associations, magazines covering your profession or industry, newspapers, classified ads and job advertisements, individuals currently working in similar jobs in the same industry, and executive recruiters. In most cases all you need do is ask if the information is available. Executive recruiters or "head hunters" are a great source, as those specializing in your area of interest are dealing with salaries day in and day out and have nothing to lose by giving you accurate information which is more current than anything published.

● HOW TO HANDLE THE NEGOTIATIONS

Let's look at a hypothetical situation. You have been alerted that an offer is about to be made. Now the PE will probably ask you, "What is your present salary level?" or "How much were they paying you at the XYZ Company?" or "What compensation do you require?," or maybe just, "How much do you want?" You should preface your answer by telling the PE that you researched compensation for the job, size of company, and geographical area before the interview. Then your pitch might go like this: "The American Psychological Association 2000 Survey shows a salary range from $47,000 to $53,000 per year, with a median figure of $49,000 per year. I believe you're looking for quality, or you wouldn't be seeing me in the first place. Therefore, I think that $X is fair. Agreed?" The X should be 15–20% above the salary range you have decided on earlier. And of course, the figures you quote from the survey should support your opener.

Another basis for negotiation available to every job hunter is the mythical offer. It can be used either by itself or in conjunction with your researched salary figures. If a PE asks you your present salary or desired compensation, say, "Well, I already have an offer at $X." If the PE balks at the "offer," real or mythical, you can back it up with the statement about your salary research. As long as you haven't priced yourself out of the market, the PE will begin to negotiate with you.

Sometimes I am asked the obvious question: Why not lie about your present salary, making it much higher than it actually is and negotiate from there? I do not recommend this. Aside from any ethical considerations, it is easy for a PE to find out your actual salary if he wants to. A surprisingly large number of companies will release this information to anyone who claims to have a need to know. Some "friends" from former companies will gleefully give a formal denial when asked to confirm the figure you have stated to your PE. Or the PE could ask you to produce a W-2 withholding form or even your federal income tax return. Then, of course, there are agencies that specialize in background checks. Ergo, lying about your present salary is not recommended.

If for some reason you are forced into revealing your current salary, there are acceptable tactics you can use to enhance your salary picture. You can give a figure that includes an expected salary increase. For example, if your annual raises have been averaging 10 percent over the last few years, you can add that expected 10 percent. Or you can include the dollar value of fringe benefits such as bonus, car, and stock options.

● WHY YOU SHOULDN'T GIVE YOUR ACTUAL BOTTOMLINE FIGURE IMMEDIATELY

Negotiations require a good deal of "indirection" and patience. After the strain of a vigorous job campaign and the stress of the interview, many job hunters feel great relief and goodwill knowing that they are about to get an offer. As a result, they want to be direct and have done with it. "Look," they would like to tell the PE, "I know you want me, and you know I would like to come to work for you. I need $X per year in order to do this."

Such directness is generally a mistake. Even if you really have only one salary figure in mind, do not give it immediately. If you do, you surrender all psychological advantages to the PE. Any additional negotiating, for example, moving expenses and other conditions of employment may be difficult to negotiate. He will expect an immediate figure for that as well. Many PEs enjoy negotiating and may not be as eager as you to conclude the deal. If you cite your actual salary figure up front, the PE will start to negotiate from there—and he will expect the bargaining process to be downward, never upward.

More than likely, your real salary goal consists of two figures which you developed from your salary research. The first is the highest figure you can hope to achieve; the second is the minimum you would accept. Unless you know your top figure is way above what he can pay, and yet you still want the job, start out at 15 to 20% above your top figure. You never know what is going to happen, and you can always come down.

A friend of mind had an acceptable range once of a minimum of $90,000 a year and $120,000 that was the most he could hope to achieve. After negotiating for awhile without mentioning a figure, his prospective boss said, "Okay, I think we're ready to talk turkey. How much do you want?" My friend added $20,000 to his top figure which was still within the range of the job from his research. "My research indicates that $140,000 would be a fair figure for someone of my abilities," he said. Remember, even though his research did indicate that $140,000 was at the top of the range, he expected that $120,000 was the most he would be able to negotiate, and he was willing to accept as little as $90,000.

"Done," his new boss said, and reached out his hand to close the deal. You never do know what's going to happen. But had his prospective boss balked at the high figure, he would have asked how much he had expected to pay, and continued to negotiate.

● WHAT TO DO WHEN THE PE COUNTERS YOUR SALARY OPENER

Let's review where we are. During pre-negotiations you gave some broad hints about salary without giving an exact figure or mentioning salary directly. During the interview, when you realized that you had made a sale, you stated a specific salary to negotiate from. This figure was 15 to 20% above the top of your range. Several things can happen at this point:

- The PE may name a salary figure within your range that you find acceptable.
- The PE may counter with a salary at the lower end of your range (or below it) that you are not ready to accept at this time.
- The PE may state his own salary range, which may or may not overlap yours.
- Finally, the PE may defer a decision, stating that he must discuss the matter with his staff, and ask you to return for another meeting later.

If the PE names an acceptable salary, you can either stop negotiating or continue to negotiate for more. You could, for example, tell the PE that you feel the job is worth at least $X (a figure 10 percent higher than the PE's offer). The decision to continue negotiating calls for careful judgment, and only you, on the spot, can make it. However, you should know that few PEs will eliminate you because you asked for 10 percent more, and you should keep in mind that not infrequently an annual salary increase may be no more than 5 percent at best.

If the PE counters with a range, your target is of course the top figure of that range. Chances are you will not be able to get more than the top figure. However, if your minimum acceptable salary is above this, now is the time to say so. Tell the PE that the job appears very challenging and you feel you would enjoy working for the company; however, you already have an offer for $X (a figure 10 to 20 percent higher than your minimum acceptable figure). If he immediately counters with a figure which is higher, but still below your minimum acceptable figure, tell him that you feel the minimum acceptable salary taking all factors into consideration is $Y (a figure X percent above your minimum). You will leave room for further negotiations without going below your minimum acceptable figure, and you may still get more than your minimum amount.

If the PE refuses to move into your acceptable range, thank him for his offer and tell him you are unable to accept. Let him know that you are still very interested in the job, and ask him to contact you in the next week or so if there is any way that the salary level can be increased. If the PE says that it is impossible to go higher, try to make up the difference by negotiating for fringe benefits above the standard package offered.

In addition to salary, you can try negotiating for a company automobile, an expense account, club memberships, a bonus, or stock options. You might also consider more frequent salary reviews or an initial review after three to six months. Sometimes even though the PE cannot increase the basic salary for the job, he can increase the fringe benefits, so this approach is more than worthwhile.

If an impasse occurs, tell the PE that you'd like a few days to think the situation over. Using the techniques described earlier in the book, make an appointment for an additional meeting on the spot. Before you return for the second round, think up several additional arguments to support your minimum acceptable figure. If the PE appears uninterested at this point, or if you sense that he will not change his stated (unacceptable) offer and will not or cannot negotiate fringe benefits, it is best to thank him, break off negotiations, and not waste any more of your time.

What if the top figure of the PE's range is within your range? The situation is similar to that of the previous offer, except that you now have a top figure which you can accept. However, the PE may be willing to go higher, so you should keep negotiating. Again, you can cite a mythical offer.

I sometimes get asked about mythical offers. First, are they ethical? I believe they are. As a friend of mine who teaches negotiating says, "A lie is not a lie when the truth is not expected." What he is talking about is the fact that few expect total factual accuracy when negotiating. You may have seen examples of this yourself on TV news reports of strikes. The reporter questions a representative of either labor or management about the other side's latest offer. "Unconscionable. We can't live with it. We will never accept it." The next day there are smiles all around. The offer has been accepted. That's negotiating. No one points out that "the facts" stated by either side or both sides turned out to be false. And the company is still profitable and the workers still earn a living—even though this was stated to be "impossible" only a few hours previously.

Job hunters also want to know, "What if they ask me the name of the companies that made the mythical offers?" You don't need to tell your PE everything they ask. The PE really doesn't expect an answer to a question like this. Just smile and say, "That's proprietary and competitive information."

Okay, so tell the PE that you already have an offer at $X (the PE's *top* figure). In response, the PE may meet or even better the mythical offer. At worst, he will probably continue negotiating.

Why Harriet C.'s Husband Was Mad At Me— But Not Afterwards

Harriet C. was one of my first students. She learned her lessons well. Within eight months after my course she had a senior position with a well-known company. Several years later, she quit work and went back to school full time to get her MBA from one of the top ten business schools in the country.

Several months later, she called. "I used the sales letter campaign again, however, I want to be a management consultant with a major firm in this area. There weren't that many PEs to mail to. Anyway, I got an interview with _____ (a prestigious management consulting company). I had a series of good interviews, and they made the offer yesterday. My PE told me they were going overboard to get me and made an offer of $40,000. (Now, you have to understand that $40,000 was a lot on money in those days. It probably translates to about $100,000 a year today. In fact, that year $40,000 a year was among the top 1% offered to new MBAs.) I asked him if he could do any better, and he told me that $40,000 was the absolute maximum."

"Why do you want more," I asked. "$40,000 sounds pretty good."

"Well, said Harriet, I read in *Business Week* that a graduate of Harvard Business School got $50,000 this year. I should be able to do the same. Anyway, I took your advice. I told him I really thought his company was tops and I really wanted to work for him. However, I have two other offers at more money, so I would have to think it over."

"Are they real?" I asked.

"No," Harriet replied, "They're mythical offers. And my husband is really mad at you. $40,000 a year is more money than he makes as a chemical engineer, and he's been working for ten years. He said I should have taken the $40,000."

"What are you supposed to do now?"

"Well, I'm supposed to get back to them tomorrow. What should I do?"

"Don't worry," I said. "You're in great shape. When you go in tomorrow, tell him again how much you want to work for him. But than say, 'But one of my offers is at $47,500. Will you meet that offer?'"

"What if he says 'no'?" asked Harriet.

"Then just pause for several seconds as if you were thinking . . . say, 'I wouldn't do this except that I really want to work for you, so I'll take the $40,000.' If there is any chance of you getting more, you'll get it."

Harriet called me the next day. "My husband isn't mad at you any more," she exclaimed. "It happened just as you said. When I asked him if he would meet the $47,500 offer, he said, 'Harriet, I can't. The best I can do is $45,000.' That's when I almost screwed up. I jumped up and said, 'I'll take it.'"

Note that the PE had told Harriet earlier that $40,000 was absolute tops . . . but it turned out to be all part of the negotiation.

● WHAT TO DO AFTER YOU GET THE OFFER

Once you and the PE agree on an acceptable figure, you should confirm the offer: "Let me see if I understand the offer correctly. Annual salary will be at $X with the following fringe benefits . . . ." Write it all down in your notebook. Tell the PE you would like a couple of days to consider the offer and will let him know by a specific date. This will allow you to conclude the interview with an offer in your pocket. A PE will rarely withdraw an offer, and in the interval you can reconsider all aspects of the job and wait for additional offers to mature. Of course, if you are completely satisfied, and you've been looking a long time, you can accept on the spot. Just don't make it sound too easy.

Many PEs prefer not to make an offer right away. Others may delay so that they can consider additional candidates. If your PE does not make an offer during the interview, remind the PE of your mythical offer at $X. Ask him to contact you by a specific day within a week. If you do not retain control over the hiring situation, you may find yourself on a string until the PE finds someone else. You must not allow this to happen. Maintain a sense of urgency by letting the PE know that he is in competition for your services and must act quickly.

If you are unemployed, your positive mental attitude and mental techniques are especially valuable. Clearly, your negotiating position would be stronger if you were employed and not dependent on finding a job. However, you can make your negotiating position appear just as strong or stronger by convincing the PE that you have another offer at a competitive salary.

If salary discussions are postponed and you receive an offer by phone, use the techniques described earlier in this chapter to conclude negotiations. You may also receive an offer by mail. If it isn't satisfactory, you can open negotiations by calling and asking for another interview; should distance make this impossible, you can negotiate by telephone.

● HOW TO NEGOTIATE WITH SEVERAL PES SIMULTANEOUSLY

If you have several offers going at the same time, you are in an ideal position. Don't hesitate to play one PE against the other, as long as you maintain your dignity. Do not become arrogant, and do not actually accept an offer. Once you accept an offer, you should shut off all negotiations.

Sometimes after a job candidate has accepted one offer, another PE will counter with an offer that is significantly higher. The lesson here is that there is a lot of room for negotiation before accepting a salary offer. For example, Larry L. had a successful interview and was told he would receive an offer by mail.

Larry understood that the offer would be approximately $30,000 a year. $30,000 was Larry's salary goal, so he was pretty happy. The next day Larry had an interview with another firm and received an on-the-spot offer of $35,000.

After thinking things through, Larry decided to accept the second offer, since it met his salary objective and offered other advantages. In the meantime he received an offer from the first PE in the mail, at $30,000 as expected. Larry called the second PE and accepted that offer. He then called the first PE to let him know. The PE immediately countered by offering $40,000.

If you accept one offer and afterward receive a significantly better deal from someone else, you've got a decision to make. If one offer is really that much better, few PEs will stand in your way. However, many (I am one) feel that once you actually accept an offer, that's it. Negotiations are over. If you get a better offer afterwards, too bad. You should have kept negotiating. However, I'm not going to judge you if you want the higher offer after having accepted a lower one. Tell the PE who made the "significantly better" offer that your acceptance (if that is your decision) is contingent on being released from your previous obligation.

● WHERE THE HIGHER SALARIES ARE

As a rule, larger companies can afford to pay the highest salaries. However, such companies may be more rigid than smaller firms in negotiating salary and fringe benefits. Smaller companies may offer very competitive salaries when they need a candidate's services immediately. Salary policies can vary widely, so never take a particularly low salary offer as a personal insult or as a final figure. Try to negotiate an acceptable figure; if you can't, move on.

To negotiate the highest salary possible, always be pleasant and courteous and maintain a positive mental attitude. If you research salary carefully and use the other techniques described in this chapter, you will be able to negotiate a great salary in line with your great job.

The Main Point

Do your salary research, and always negotiate the offer.

APPENDIX A

SAMPLE ADVERTISEMENTS AND ANALYSES OF RESPONSES

● RESPONSE TO AN ADVERTISEMENT FOR AN R&D MANAGER

Senior R&D Manager

Highly technical Ohio firm is looking for a senior manager of chemical research. Should have 10 to 15 years of experience managing process and development chemistry in a research lab. Must have strong management background and excellent communications skills. Compensation is commensurate with experience. Outstanding fringe benefits. If you are interested in this position, please submit your resume and salary history in confidence to. . . .

This advertisement has three stated requirements: (1) 10 to 15 years of experience managing process and development chemistry in a research lab; (2) a strong management background; and (3) excellent communications skills.

Through the telephone, let's assume that you have learned the following additional information: the position reports to the vice president of research and development, who feels that good R&D chemists publish. He is proud of the recognition given to members of his division, who received several patents as well as awards from organizations. You have also learned that communication is a major part of the job. In the past, top management has been suspicious of research programs. Every program has had to be thoroughly written up and sold through a formal presentation by the senior R&D manager.

The response to this ad should be written exactly like your sales letter, starting with an attention getter and ending with a call to action. Here is a sample letter:

As product research manager in a rapidly growing company, my success rate for new product development is 57%. This is better than twice the success rate of 5 other product research managers in my company.

I am writing in response to your advertisement for a senior manager of chemical research. I meet all your stated requirements.

10 to 15 Years of Experience Managing Process and Development Chemistry in a Research Lab

In 14 years of managing both process and developmental chemistry, I have:

- Directed the development of 37 new products and 17 processes that resulted in $250 million in sales potential.
- Managed development of the "physical fitness pill," judged one of the top 100 inventions of the year 1998 by *Industrial Research Magazine*.
- Been awarded 17 patents, with 5 patents pending.

Strong managerial background

- Led and directed research organizations from members to multi-disciplined groups totaling 27 chemical engineers, research scientists, and medical technicians.
- Headed the new products division of the Xerox Company. Responsible for staffing, planning, budgeting, and scheduling as well as technical output and supervision of 18 chemical engineers, including 7 Ph.D.s.

Excellent Communications Skills

- Authored 12 papers published in technical journals in 4 countries.
- Gave 14 technical presentations to such organizations as the American Chemical Society and the International Society of Developmental Chemists.
- Over a 14-year period, made 71 presentations on results and proposals to customers, potential customers, and top management with an 81% rate of proposal acceptance.

I have a BS and MS in chemical engineering from New York University.

I would be happy to discuss further details of my experience in a personal interview.

Now you are probably thinking that this candidate is uniquely, incredibly, suited to the job. After all, look at the statistics: 57% success rare, $250 million in sales potential, 71 presentations. But stop and think a minute. Have you ever sat down and worked out your own success rate? How many total dollars in sales potential have you been responsible for? If your job requires presentations, how many have you made during your career? The answers to these questions may surprise you. They represent the kinds of accomplishments you should develop and include in your resume for ready reference.

● RESPONSE TO AN ADVERTISEMENT FOR AN INTERNATIONAL ATTORNEY

International Attorney

New York-based division of a Fortune 500 corporation seeks attorney with 2 to 3 years of major law firm training in corporate and commercial law and litigation to fill important staff position. Duties will span domestic and international operations and will include some travel. Ability to deal at a high negotiator level, ability to draft sophisticated agreements, and excellent academic and professional background is mandatory. Fluency in Spanish required. Superior opportunity offering immediate responsibility and upward mobility. Generous salary and benefits plan. All replies will be treated as confidential. Forward resume to. . . .

This advertisement has five stated requirements: (1) 2 to 3 years of major law firm training in corporate and commercial law and litigation; (2) an ability to deal at a high negotiator level; (3) an ability to draft sophisticated agreements; (4) excellent academic and professional records, and (5) fluency in Spanish.

In addition, the ad contains an unstated "requirement" that will greatly assist any candidate in getting an interview. It is implied by the headline of the advertisement and by the second sentence: "Duties will span domestic and international operations and will include some travel." If you have had any international experience, especially in a Spanish-speaking country, you should definitely work this into your response with at least one accomplishment.

Again, through contact over the telephone, let's assume you discover that the PE deals primarily in the cosmetics industry. Unless you have cosmetics industry experience, you should not specify the industry in which you worked in your response. Naturally, if you have such experience, you should emphasize it. You have also learned that youth is important. The PE wants someone no older than 35. If you are under 35, you should state your age clearly in your letter.

Here is a sample response:

I was commended by the general manager for "an outstanding job of negotiating and saving the company at least $3 million" when I went to Spain and negotiated a $30 million settlement for my firm.

My letter is in response to your advertisement for an international attorney. I meet all the requirements stated in your advertisement.

2 Years of Major Law Firm Training in Corporate and Commercial Law and Litigation

- In 2 years in a major Chicago law firm, I assisted in handling 13 separate cases involving commercial law and litigation with 8 different corporate clients.

Ability to Deal at a High Negotiator Level.

- I participated in 10 major negotiations for a major manufacturing company with more than $500 million in annual sales.
- Although only 31 years old, I was chief negotiator for a $30 million settlement with a foreign company headquartered in Spain.

Ability to Draft Sophisticated Agreements

- Drafted 16 separate contractual agreements involving a potential $58 million in royalties and other settlements.
- Drafted a 125-page contract in Spanish.

Excellent Academic and Professional Background

- I have a BA in business administration from the University of Illinois (1991) with an A average.
- I am an honors graduate JDS from the University of Chicago (1997).
- I am a member of the Illinois bar.

Fluency in Spanish

- I am fluent in Spanish reading, writing, and speaking—and have negotiated in Spanish as well as English.

I would be happy to meet with you at your convenience to discuss my background in detail.

● RESPONSE TO AN ADVERTISEMENT FOR A MANUFACTURING MANAGER

Manufacturing Manager

We are an expanding Los Angeles-based company in the energy industry. We manufacture a small volume of sophisticated electromechanical hardware for use in our service business and seek the right individual to run our manufacturing department. The manager we are seeking will have 15 to 20 years of manufacturing management experience and should possess undergraduate technical and graduate business degrees. Experience should include responsible positions in materials control, production control, and scheduling, in addition to at least one year of total manufacturing responsibility. Familiarity with electronics and electromechanical applications is essential. Please send resume and salary history to. . . .

This advertisement contains five straightforward requirements: (1) 15 to 20 years of manufacturing management experience: (2) undergraduate technical and graduate business degrees; (3) responsible positions in materials control, production control, and scheduling; (4) at least one year of total manufacturing responsibility; and (5) familiarity with electronics and electromechanical applications.

Also important to the executive job hunter is the information contained in the first three lines: "We manufacture a small volume of sophisticated electromechanical hardware." If you have manufacturing experience with small-volume, sophisticated electromechanical equipment, emphasize this fact. If not, say nothing.

If you do not meet all the requirements, should you still answer the ad? Definitely yes. Many times PEs overstate their requirements because they lack knowledge of the potential employees that are available, because they have an idealized view of what it takes to be a success in the job, or because they believe that overstating requirements will get them the best responses. Frequently the individual who is hired does not meet all the stated requirements of the ad. So if you feel you are qualified for a job even though you do not meet every requirement, you should respond. Of course, do not state that you meet all the requirements in your letter (but don't say that you do not meet them either).

Let's say that Hank wants to apply for the job of manufacturing manager described above. Hank graduated with BS in electrical engineering from the University of Florida in 1980. His first job was as a design engineer in a large aerospace company. After two years he transferred to manufacturing and was put in charge of materials control. He directed a number of projects concerned with low-volume, sophisticated electromechanical hardware. He was promoted twice in the next three years. By 1985, he was deputy electromechanical manufacturing manager.

During this time Hank started going to night school, and by mid-1985 he had finished all his course work except a thesis for his MBA. Then recession struck the aerospace industry, and Hank was laid off. Within a few months Hank was working again, this time as production control manager for a small electronics company making high-volume electronic components. In 1992 Hank was promoted to manufacturing manager. A few years later he realized that for various political reasons he would not be promoted and began looking for a new job.

Now consider Hank's situation. He has almost 20 years of manufacturing management experience, three years in low-volume, sophisticated electromechanical hardware. He has a technical undergraduate degree and has completed his course work for an MBA. Hank has held responsible positions in materials control and production control, but has had little direct experience (other than as manufacturing manager) with scheduling. He has two years of total manufacturing responsibility as well as a familiarity with electronics and electromechanical applications. Here is a letter Hank could have written in response to the previous ad:

> As manufacturing manager for a company manufacturing electronic components, I direct all aspects of production, including materials control, production control, and scheduling. I cut production costs by 15 percent while increasing output by 22 percent.
>
> I am writing in response to your advertisement for a manufacturing manager. Here are some of the highlights of my experience.

15 to 20 Years of Manufacturing Management Experience

> I have 18 years of manufacturing management experience, ranging from a small company (Advanced Electronic Products Co., Inc.) to a major aerospace company (Douglas Aircraft Company). I have directed the production of small-volume, highly sophisticated electromechanical hardware for actuators, electronic sensing devices, and electronic components.

Undergraduate Technical and Graduate Business Degrees

> I have a BS in electrical engineering from the University of Florida and all course work completed for an MBA from the University of California.

Responsible Positions in Materials Control, Production Control, and Scheduling

> - Responsible for materials control in the manufacture of low-volume, highly sophisticated electromechanical hardware. Saved my company more than $2 million over a three-year period. Promoted twice in three years. Was deputy electromechanical manufacturing manager at age 28.
> - Headed production control for a small firm. Reorganized production control department. Developed a sequence of scheduling and manufacturing that saved the company $50,000 per year in manufacturing costs with developed products and $25,000 per year with products developed after the sequence was implemented.
> - Promoted to manufacturing manager at age 33 on retirement of former manufacturing manager.

At Least One Year of Total Manufacturing Responsibility

> - Total manufacturing responsibility for 2½ years.
> - Responsible for all functions of manufacturing operation, including production control, inventory control, materials control, scheduling, maintaining quality.

Familiarity with Electronics and Electromechanical Application

- 12 years of experience in electronics-related industries.
- 10 years of experience in electromechanical hardware and electronic component manufacturing management.
- 2 years of experience in the design of electromechanical hardware and subsystems.

As I am currently employed as a manufacturing manager, please keep this information confidential. I will, of course, be happy to meet with you to discuss further details of my experience.

● RESPONSE TO AN ADVERTISEMENT FOR A VICE PRESIDENT

Vice President

This key position, reporting to the president of a major NYSE company based in Denver, demands the skills and intellect of a true professional. The successful candidate should currently be running a successful profit center, hold an MBA from a top-rated university, have a demonstrated fast track record, and be considered highly promotable. Strengths should encompass manufacturing (preferably electromechanical devices) and in-depth knowledge of marketing and cost controls/finance. Chief responsibilities will be monitoring the performance of four of this firm's divisions. Judgment will play an important role in this position, as well as the ability to spot trends and encourage or reverse them. Reply in confidence with resume and salary history to Mr. Jim Bates, International Executive Search Associates.

In this advertisement the executive recruiter has identified himself, so there should be no difficulty obtaining additional information about the job.

Assume that in calling Jim Bates you learn that over the past year two of the four division general managers have been replaced. One of these divisions is still losing money. The average age of the general managers is 43. The president feels that a more experienced executive, preferably with a manufacturing, marketing, or financial background and an MBA, is needed to get things turned around. Currently the president runs all eight of the company's divisions, with three other company officers holding staff positions in production, marketing, and finance. The position of vice president is a new one.

The company is a conglomerate. Four of its divisions are in some facet of the metal-processing industry. These divisions would still be run by the president. The other four divisions are involved in electronics. One division is devoted entirely to electronic defense products; another manufactures various types of alarm systems; the remaining two manufacture small, high-volume electronic equipment. These divisions would be run by the new vice president.

Try your own hand at drafting a reply to this ad. Then go over the following checklist to see if you have covered all the bases.

In completing your response, did you make a list of the requirements in the ad, both stated and implied, and a list of additional requirements obtained in talking with Jim Bates? Your list should include the following:

Stated Requirements

Currently running a successful profit center.

Hold an MBA from a top-rated university.

Have a demonstrated fast-track record.

Be considered highly promotable.

Strength in manufacturing (preferably electromechanical devices).

In-depth knowledge of marketing and cost controls/finance.

Implied Requirements

Ability or past experience in monitoring performance of several divisions.

Ability to spot trends as well as to encourage or reverse them.

Requirements or Desirable Experience through Talking with Jim Bates

Past experience in turning around an unprofitable operation.

Manufacturing, marketing, or financial background.

Older executive.

Experience in the electronics industry, specifically with the Department of Defense, alarm systems, or small, high-volume electronic equipment.

In your response did you open with an attention-getting paragraph and write an explanation paragraph? Did you list each requirement separately, with qualifications and accomplishments supporting each one? Did you quantify your accomplishments in dollars or percentages? Did you close by calling the PE to action?

APPENDIX B

How to Find Prospective Employers

Chapter 6 already includes a couple of million potential leads under the heading "How to Develop a Mailing or E-mail List of PEs." But by going to the online job sites you can find several million more. However, remember you are supposed to break the rules. So, don't do what everyone else does. Don't go to these sites to post your resume. That's a waste of time in most cases. Also, if a PE you happen to write to, or are actually in negotiations with, happens to see it, it devalues your product. And recall, your product is you!

You don't need to send resumes or salary information to these job ads, either. Find out who the PE is by name using the techniques I've explained and contact that individual by letter, e-mail, fax, or telephone. Never, never, never send a resume.

With that in mind, here are some leading online job sites which will give you several million more opportunities on which to use the techniques, break the rules, and get a great job fast.:

http://www.careerbuilder.com

http://www.careers.wsj.com

http://www.careermosaic.com

http://www.careerpath.com

http://www.ceoexpress.com

http://www.classifieds.yahoo.com/employment.html

http://www.cweb.com

http://www.dice.com

http://www.execunet.com

http://www.headhunter.net

http://www.hotjobs.com

http://www.joboptions.com

http://www.jobsearch.org

http://www.monster.com

http://www.nationjob.com

http://www.net-temps.com

http://www.occ.com

APPENDIX C

SAMPLE INTERVIEW-GETTING LETTERS

Note that in the letters that are in this appendix, every individual appears exceptional and much better than any potential competitors. This is because unlike others, the writers of these letters took the time to review their own backgrounds in depth to uncover, document, and quantify their greatest accomplishments relevant to the positions they sought. In order to be successful, you must do the same. Writing an effective sales letter cannot be accomplished in a few minutes. This is a project that will take hours. Moreover, your letter should be polished again and again over several days until you get it just right and for maximum impact.

If it doesn't bring you the results you should get, you must rework it. Consider why it isn't working. First, before you change anything, is it going to the right target market? That is, do the individuals that you are addressing hold the correct title . . . the individual you would report to when hired and who has the authority to hire you? If not, adjust your target market.

Once you have confirmed you are sending your letter to the correct market, you should consider the contents of your letter. Are your accomplishments relevant to the job you seek? Does your headline have sufficient impact to gain your prospect's attention? Are your words short, direct, and to the point? Have you quantified each of your accomplishments? Are your grammar and spelling 100% correct?

Use the following letters as guides.

SAMPLE SALES LETTER OF A GENERAL MANAGER

Dear Mr. _____ :

As vice president and general manager of a division of a Fortune 500 corporation, I doubled sales from $10 million to $20 million in 5 years.

I am writing to you because you may be in need of someone with my experience and capabilities as general manager of one of your divisions. If this is the case, you may be interested in some of my other accomplishments.

As assistant general manager, I assumed full responsibility for one year during the illness of the general manager. In this period I successfully introduced a new product while increasing profits by 30% over the previous year.

As director of sales, I developed the first comprehensive training program for salesmen. This program assisted in increasing sales by 45% over an 18-month period.

As general manager, I directed the activities of 475 people in production, sales, research and development, engineering, finance, quality control, and personnel. During the 5 years that I held this position, sales and profits were the highest in the history of this 15-year-old division.

As district sales manager, I increased sales by 500% over a 4-year period through the 11 direct salesmen whom I personally trained.

As assistant to the president of a major corporation, I directed operation studies of four different operating divisions, including analysis of present operations, forecasts, and recommendations. I was commended by the president for "the finest example of profitable staff work I have ever seen."

I have a BS in mechanical engineering from the University of Ohio (1980) and an MBA from New York University (1982).

I look forward to meeting with you in a personal interview.

Sincerely,

Tel. No. (459) 767-9834

SAMPLE SALES LETTER OF A MARKET RESEARCH ANALYST

Dear Ms. _____ :

As market research analyst for a well-known market research firm, I directed the largest market research study ever conducted in the dairy industry, involving 42 metropolitan areas in 35 states. This study saved the client over $1 million within 1 year of completion and will ultimately save more than $10 million.

I am writing in case you are in need of a market research analyst in your current operations. Here are some other things I have done:

- Principal analyst. Was principal analyst for more than 50 research studies during a 3-year period. Coordinated the activities of 20 part-time field researchers and 3 junior analysts while doing $300,000 in market research sales.

- Marketing researcher. Participated as staff member of major aerospace company in 5 studies of future weapon systems and competitor capabilities to build similar systems. Was promoted twice in one year for "major accomplishments in assigned responsibilities."

- Publications and presentations. Authored 9 papers published in professional journals of marketing. Two papers were presented at national meetings of the American Marketing Association.

I have a BA specializing in marketing research from Amherst College (1995).

It would be my pleasure to meet with you to discuss further details of my experience.

Sincerely,

Tel. No. (343) 323–8643

SAMPLE SALES LETTER OF AN ACCOUNTING MANAGER

Dear Mr. _____ :

As controller for a medium-size engineering company, I installed a standard cost system that has saved more than $3 million over a 5-year period.

Your company may need an executive to assume responsibility for the accounting control function. If so, you may be interested in some of my other achievements.

As plant controller, I was responsible for all accounting activities, including financial statement preparation, cash administration, filing of corporate tax returns, and accounting for receivables, payables, and property. Total financial responsibility exceeded $20 million *per* year.

As assistant divisional controller of a large company, I directed all accounting activities, including statement preparation and product profit/loss analysis. I supervised operation of IBM equipment and developed an advanced budget system that is still (10 years later) in use in this company.

As chief accountant in a small company, I supervised the activities of the accounting department. I developed and installed standard material prices and labor rates, analyzed all contracts for profitability, and developed overhead rates. I was commended by the president for "increasing our finance efficiency by 1000%."

As consultant-accountant, I performed general audit work for nearly every kind of business enterprise and public and private institution. I installed 12 different systems of financial and cost controls. I progressed from assistant consultant to full consultant in less than 2 years—a first-time accomplishment in this firm.

I have a BA in accounting from the University of Oklahoma.

I would very much like to meet you personally so that we can discuss my background in more detail with a view to my becoming your accounting manager.

Sincerely,

Tel. (617) 324-0971

SAMPLE SALES LETTER OF A PUBLIC RELATIONS MANAGER

Dear Ms. _____:

In ten years of public relations work I have had 225 articles published in industrial magazines, professional journals, and trade papers, resulting in an estimated $2.5 million of publicity for my employers.

My purpose in writing this letter to you is to determine your need for a public relations manager of my capability for your firm. Here are a few of my accomplishments:

- Directed participation in 34 trade shows in 4 industries. Won seven awards for top exhibits.
- Edited 3 internal newspapers with circulations ranging from 1,500 to 55,000.
- Gave more than 100 interviews to journalists and news people.
- Developed and directed 44 individual publicity campaigns for different purposes, including new product introduction, entrance into new business, and company image improvement.
- Organized the company visit of 57 groups of dignitaries, including three foreign heads of state.
- Taught 18 courses in writing, public relations, journalism, and publicity in 2 companies and 3 different universities.

I have a BA and MA in journalism, specializing in public relations, from California State College at Fullerton.

If my background interests you, I would be happy to meet with you to give you more details in a personal interview.

Sincerely,

Tel. (202) 764-0089

FOLLOWING ARE LETTERS FROM STUDENTS JUST COMPLETING UNDERGRADUATE AND GRADUATE DEGREES

Dear Mr. _____:

I averaged 45 face-to-face interviews per week for the United States Census Bureau.

I am writing to you in case you are looking for someone as an assistant marketing researcher. If so, I have also:

> Conducted 128 telephone interviews.
>
> Designed, pretested, and revised a 40-item questionnaire used for a consumer demand study that resulted in 520 responses out of 1,000.
>
> Compiled, tabulated, and performed statistical analysis on data gathered from the field in 3 major studies.
>
> Achieved a 97 percent success rate in obtaining answers to sensitive questions.
>
> Designed, conducted, and analyzed the final results of a $14,000 unobtrusive observational survey.

I will receive a Bachelor of Science degree in marketing from the University of Missouri, Columbia, in December.

I would like very much to have a face-to-face interview with you.

Sincerely,

(314) 555-4116

Dear Ms. _____ :

I covered and wrote 107 stories for high school and university papers.

I am writing in case you need a junior reporter for your newspaper. If you do, you may be interested in some other things I have done that are relevant:

- My story on university housing practices was picked up by a major newspaper with a circulation of over 300,000.
- I received the Gold Star Quill award for being the top reporter for the university newspaper.
- While still a college sophomore, I succeeded in writing stories based on the interviews I conducted with the top 5 politicians in my state.
- As vice president of Ohio State University's Journalism Club, I recruited 21 national figures as guest speakers.

I will be graduating from Ohio State University at Columbus this month with a B.A. degree in journalism.

I would very much like to meet you face to face to discuss further the details of my background and experience. Please contact me at (614) 555-2897, 4:30 to 9:30 p.m. eastern standard time.

Sincerely,

Dear Ms. _____ :

I developed a new technique for teaching penmanship that has been adopted by 7 schools and is being taught to more than 3,000 students.

I am writing to you in case you need an elementary school teacher. If you do, you may be interested in other things I have done:

- As a teacher's aide, I assisted in teaching 6 different classes in 7 schools. I received ratings of good to outstanding from 9 supervising teachers and staff evaluators.
- While still in college, I wrote an article, "Teaching to Write Eight," for elementary teachers.
- I successfully taught crafts and good citizenship to an average of 216 campers for 3 years at Camp Sam during the summers of 2000, '01, and '02.
- I received an award for the best presentation while teaching a communication class, in the Fall of 2000.

I will be completing my Bachelor of Arts degree in education at Auburn University in May.

Can we meet to further discuss the details of my experience and your needs?

Sincerely,

(205) 555-1475

Dear Mr. _____ :

I have acted as both a Chinese and a Japanese language interpreter for 7 different groups of foreign businessmen from 3 Asian countries.

I am writing in case you need an oriental language correspondent or interpreter. if you do, you may be interested in other things I have done along these lines:

- Graded fluent in Japanese, Mandarin, and Cantonese Chinese under U.S. State Department exams in reading, writing, and comprehension.
- Traveled extensively in 12 different countries in Asia and attended for one year a Japanese school in Tokyo, Japan.
- Have maintained correspondence in 2 dialects of Chinese and Japanese with 8 different correspondents.
- Worked one summer with the East Wind Trading Agency as an interpreter and correspondent. Translated 43 different letters and documents either from Japanese into English or from English into Japanese.

I will be completing my bachelor's degree in oriental languages from UCLA at the end of May.

I would like to meet you to discuss further the details about my background in a personal interview.

Sincerely,

(213) 555-0724

Dear Dr. _____ :

I prepared a 278-page technical manual, as part of a government contract, in less than one month while working part-time.

I am writing to you in case you need a technical writer. If you do, you may be interested in other things I have done that are relevant to this position:

Authored 3 technical articles based on interviews with experts in the areas represented.

Developed and wrote advertising copy for 11 different technical products for major U.S. companies as part of a course in technical writing.

Consulted with and assisted faculty of the University of Maryland in developing 7 different proposals for grants in technical areas.

As a member of the Technical Writers Club, wrote copy, brochures, and posters that assisted in attracting 37 new members in a single semester.

I will be graduating with a B.A. degree in English literature from the University of Maryland this month.

I would like to meet you to discuss further the details of my qualifications and experience as a technical writer. You can reach me at (301) 555-8250.

Sincerely,

Dear. Mr. _____ :

At Mike's Auto, I sold 921 used cars in 7 months.

I am writing to you in the hope that you might be interested in someone with my capabilities as a used car salesman. If you are, here are some other things I've done that might interest you:

> At Right Auto, I made $5,000 in commissions one summer selling tires, brakes, shocks, etc.
>
> At S. Motors, I was a sales associate and responsible for finding leads. I averaged 5 leads a day while working part-time for more than 8 months.
>
> At Huntington College, I coordinated a fund-raising drive for the Distributive Education Clubs of America that raised $9,400.

Currently, I am attending the University of Denver where I am majoring in finance. I am seeking a part-time position so I can continue my education. I would be happy to discuss my qualifications with you in a face-to-face interview.

Sincerely,

Telephone: (303) 555-3297

Dear. Mr. _____ :

While working at a major department store, I exceeded my daily sales goal by an average of 50 percent.

I am writing to you in case you are in need of a sales representative. If you are, here are some of my other accomplishments that might interest you:

- At Oldening Industries, I helped launch their first direct-mail campaign by personally contacting 2,117 companies. This doubled our mailing list.
- At Northern Products, I was responsible for finding jobs for 115 professional personnel after a layoff. I placed 87 employees for a 76 percent success rate by personal contact.
- At Super Pine, I reduced the percentage of back orders by 16 percent in 4 weeks.

I will be graduating in June from the School of Business Administration at the University of Louisville with a degree in marketing.

I would very much like to meet you to discuss my background in more detail.

Sincerely,

(502) 555-7071

Dear Ms. _____ :

While in a government agency, I controlled 95 percent of the department's projects with a staff of 125.

I am writing to learn if you need an administrative assistant. If you do, you may be interested in some of the other things I have done:

As president of a professional management organization, with an allocated budget of $1,900, I planned, organized, and motivated other people to attain 30 members per quarter.

As vice president administrator of a public relations committee, I successfully promoted yearly activities by making 17 personal presentations and by writing to 59 chief executives of corporations with sales in excess of $100 million a year.

As a marketing student, I conducted 7 market research studies and consulted for a private firm.

I will graduate from the University of Illinois at Urbana-Champaign in September with a degree in marketing management.

I would be happy to meet you to discuss my background in greater detail.

Sincerely,

Telephone: (217) 555-4567

Dear Mr. _____ :

I developed a revised hiring plan for an automobile parts franchise that has the potential to decrease personnel turnover by 22 percent.

I am writing to learn if you need a personnel manager. If you do, you may be interested in some of the other things I have done:

> I was in charge of hiring for a retail store with 12 employees. While similar stores were suffering a 25 to 35 percent turnover every year, my store lost only two employees in 3 years.

> I developed a profile of highly productive retail employees for a university course. This profile was applied by 5 retailers in the local area. They reported an average productivity increase of 9 percent.

> At an experimental management clinic, I organized and motivated 26 students to perform various tasks and received the top class grade of 98 percent.

I will receive my B.S. degree in management from Texas A&M in June.

I would be happy to meet you to discuss further the details of what I have done and how it may be applied to your business.

Sincerely,

(409) 555-7607

Dear Mr. _____:

I received the dean's award for the best commercial art drawing of 2001.

I am writing to you in case you need a commercial artist. If you do, here are some other things I have accomplished that may interest you:

- Completed 9 line drawings for a new product introduced by General Motors.
- Served as head artist, University Times. Completed 23 pieces of artwork published by the University Times over a 2-year period.
- Freelanced for 2 different advertising agencies over a 3-year period. Successfully completed 12 different commercial art assignments.
- Did voluntary artwork for 4 student organizations including the development of concepts and drawings of 17 different pieces.
- Won first place in a university contest for drawing the best poster representing United Way.

I will be completing my B.A. degree in commercial art at Emporia State University this June.

I would like to meet you to discuss further the details of my qualifications as a commercial artist.

Sincerely yours,

(913) 555-1681

Dear. Mr. _____ :

I ran a 280-unit, $10 million condominium project. I am writing to you in case you are in need of a manager's assistant, budget control.

At a construction company with sales of $200 million a year, I:

Established a standard cost accounting system to control a $10 million project.

Charted cash flow of $30,000 per month.

Budgeted funds of $300,000 per year.

Directed 5 subcontractors.

Maintained liaison with 7 government officials.

Dealt with 13 customers.

Maintained bank and financial relationships.

I have a B.S. degree in civil engineering from California State University, Los Angeles, and will receive an MBA specializing in finance from Wright State University in June.

I would very much like to meet you so that we can discuss my background in more detail. I can be reached at (513) 555-5834 from 9:00 a.m. to 5:00 p.m.

Sincerely,

Dear Ms. _____ :

With an international advertising agency, I made 277 cold calls, tracked 83 leads, and conducted 18 personal interviews with small business owners for new account development.

I am writing because you may need someone with my capabilities as a business manager. If you do, you may be interested in some of my other accomplishments:

At Drakes Department Store: As a sales associate, I sold an average of $16,000 worth of women's shoes each month on a part-time basis. I also developed a stockroom management system that expedited locating merchandise. This system increased the efficiency and the productivity of each sales associate.

At California State University, Los Angeles: As an administrative management assistant, I redesigned and implemented a survey for a $6 million campus housing project. This survey was successfully distributed to 2,600 students.

In the U.S. Air Force: As a sergeant, I managed a support staff of 3 and controlled an inventory of $100,000 to $200,000 in aircraft parts per day. I also scheduled the work to be performed on 18 base aircraft.

I will have a B.S. degree in marketing from California State University, Los Angeles, in August.

I would like very much to meet you to discuss my background in more detail and review my qualifications.

Sincerely,

Telephone: (213) 555-2001

Dear Mr. _____ :

At PAC Import Company, I discovered and purchased a cube puzzle from a manufacturer in Hong Kong shortly after its introduction. As a result, PAC beat all local competition and earned $30,000 in profits.

I am writing to you in case you need a merchandise buyer. If so, you may be interested in some of my other accomplishments:

- As a part-time import buyer, I researched and recommended purchase of more than 13 successful import items resulting in sales of $297,000.
- I researched and developed a marketing plan for a retail business and planned the purchase of 5 new items with sales potential in excess of $90,000.
- I accomplished 3 major research studies on demographics and ethnic make-up of the Racine area.
- While a student, I managed a budget of $4,200 and acted as buying agent for the University of Wisconsin Drama Club.

I will be graduating from the University of Wisconsin in May with a B.A. degree in management.

I would very much like to meet you to discuss additional details of my qualifications.

Sincerely,

Telephone: (414) 555-0686

Arthur P. Rey
4512 Glen Echo Drive
Pasadena, California 91107

May 1, 2001

Ms. W.A. Jones
President
All Day Shipping, Inc.
501 4th Avenue
Long Beach, California 90009

Dear Ms. Jones:

While at Go Fast Shipping, I developed the inbound traffic department and in-creased efficiency by 30 percent, saving $13,000 in overall department costs.

I am writing because you may be interested in my qualifications and back-ground as a traffic manager:

> At Zip Trading Company, I developed a new bill of lading form that was adopted at all branch offices. Error rate was reduced an estimated 14 percent.
>
> At New Export, Inc., I reworked distribution plans and found a more effi-cient way of transporting our products that cut costs by 13 percent.
>
> While in the U.S. Navy, I was assigned to the supply department. I was commended for designing new transportation forms that increased over-all efficiency and are saving the Navy $15,000 a year.

I will receive a B.S. degree in transportation from California State University, Los Angeles, in June.

I would be happy to meet with you to discuss my background and experience in more detail.

Sincerely,

Arthur R. Rey

(213) 555-1211

John P. Matkins
507 N. Aimes Street
Tempe, Arizona 85281

November 21, 2010

Ms. S. Tomkins
Forward Financial Corporation
2013 Handler Boulevard
Phoenix, Arizona 85350

Dear Ms. Tomkins:

While at 1st National Bank of Arizona, I increased new accounts development by $1 million in 2 days.

I am writing to learn if you need a senior lending officer. If so, you may be interested in some of my other accomplishments:

- At 1st National Bank, I redesigned the lending files system. The time required to locate information decreased 23 percent. I also developed $500,000 in new loans in a month.
- As membership chairman of the Economics Club at Arizona State University, I recruited 16 student members in one hour.
- Working full-time while attending the university, I expanded the lending department 11 percent, got 100 percent participation from our staff while in charge of the United Way campaign, and organized a get-acquainted party with top management and the branch VIP customers. This effort resulted in an increase of 34 percent in branch deposits.

I will be graduating this December from the School of Business Administration, Arizona State University, Tempe, with a B.A. degree in finance.

I would like to have the opportunity to meet at your convenience to discuss in detail my qualifications and possible future with your corporation. I can be reached at (201) 555-1336.

Sincerely,

John P. Matkins

Richard B. Mann
1234th Avenue
Fayetteville, Arkansas 72701

July 9, 2004

Mr. Darryl B. Maddox
Coopers and Associates
54 Stevens Boulevard
Fayetteville, Arkansas 72701

Dear Mr. Maddox:

Responsible for oversight and checking in an accounting department, I increased output by 36 percent without loss of accuracy.

I am writing in case you are in need of an auditor. If you are, you may be interested in some of my other accomplishments:

- At Zeus Sales Company, I helped rebuild and assigned 14 general ledger accounts for the company's newly installed in-house computer. This saved the company an estimated 16 percent per year in time.
- At Lawson, Inc., I assisted independent auditors in preparing 21 audit working papers.
- In another assignment, I maintained records and journal entries for 86 employees. I assisted the controller in rebuilding general ledger accounts for the newly installed in-house computer.
- At Universal Accounts, Inc., I managed the books of a company with a $20,500 inventory and $238,450 total assets, and I was responsible for the tax liability.

I will be graduating in August from the School of Business Administration at the University of Arkansas with a Bachelor of Science degree in accounting.

I would like very much for us to meet to discuss my background in more detail.

Sincerely yours,

Richard B. Mann

(501) 555-5789

Nancy E. Block
147 Forest Drive
Philadelphia, Pennsylvania 19121

May 14, 2005

Mr. James Sparrow, President
Sparrow and Associates
157 Willow Way
Philadelphia, Pennsylvania 19122

Dear Mr. Sparrow:

I wrote advertising copy that resulted in 141 responses in one week.

I am writing in case you need an advertising copywriter. If you do, here are some other things that I have done:

> As part of an advertising course, I wrote copy for 17 full-page ads for 17 different products. I received an "A" evaluation for each one.

> I prepared 22 ads as a copywriter for a university newspaper for 7 different clients over a 2-year period. Every client requested additional advertising.

> I analyzed 51 different national ads by well-known copywriters and agencies. In every case I specified elements that worked and those that did not and correlated these with the actual results from the ads.

> I attended 5 seminars on copywriting at my own expense.

In June I will be graduating from Temple University with a B.A. degree in English.

My ambition is to be a full-time copywriter with your agency. I would very much like to meet you to discuss my experience and qualifications for this position.

Sincerely,

Nancy E. Block
Telephone: (215) 555-4805

MICHAEL GREEN
1704 Park Lane
Huntington, California 92059

December 7, 2002

Mr. William McLaughin, Branch Sales Manager
ABC Company
1234 South Street
Los Angeles, CA 12345

Dear. Mr. McLaughlin:

While at Johnson's Business Machines, I reduced the time to qualify sales leads from 66 days to 7 days.

I am writing to you in case you are in need of an information processing salesman. If so, you may be interested in some of my other accomplishments:

- Demonstrated $30,000 in equipment to 34 prospective customers.
- Trained 5 customers and their staffs on newly purchased equipment.
- Sold $18,000 worth of contracts at $36 each in less than two months.
- Developed a proposal to initiate a direct mail campaign that was accepted by top management. Estimated sales: $100,000.
- Organized, managed, and motivated 126 people to sell 18,000 Disneyland tickets for a fund-raiser that grossed $151,000.
- Represented 2,500 dorm residents to university officials.

I will be graduating this December from the School of Business Administration, University of Southern California, with a marketing management degree.

I would very much like to meet you so that we can discuss my background in more detail and review my qualifications to be a sales representative at ABC Company.

Sincerely,

Michael Green

(213) 555-2099

Joseph A. Betti
1705 South 50th Street
Chicago, Illinois 60631

May 1, 2001

Mr. John H. Steven
Executive Director
Boys Club of Chicago
17065 East 110th Street
Chicago, Illinois 60630

Dear Mr. Steven:

I worked with 102 boys in 3 different youth gangs in Chicago and organized 13 different events for them.

I am writing in case you need a youth organizer for your club. If you do, you may be interested in some other things that I have done:

As a Boy Scout, I reached the rank of Eagle Scout and was assigned duties as Junior Assistant Scoutmaster. I was totally responsible for 37 boys in 5 major scouting events, and assistant to the Scoutmaster in 22 other events.

As program event chairman for my fraternity, I organized, planned, and conducted 7 fraternity programs including a fund-raiser that raised $4,000.

During my presidency of the University Photography Club, membership grew from 17 to 47 members. My responsibilities included supervising a club newsletter, overseeing an $82,000 photography lab, and directing the activities of 3 other club officers.

At the university, I participated on the teams of 3 different sports and was elected captain of the tennis team.

I will be graduating in June from the University of Chicago with a B.A. degree in psychology. I would like to have a personal interview with you so we can discuss further the details of my background for this important position.

Sincerely,

Joseph A. Betti

Telephone: (312) 555-9021

Howard A. Spalding
7075 Austin Drive
Lubbock, Texas 79409

May 7, 2003

Mr. Albert A. Letz, Director
Department of Mechanical Engineering
High Technology Engineering Company
17705 Business Drive
Lubbock, Texas 79409

Dear Mr. Letz:

I designed 7 mechanical latches judged exceptional by an engineering professor with 30 years of experience.

I am writing in case you need a mechanical engineer for your department. If you do, you may be interested in some other things I've done along these lines:

- With two engineering classmates, built from scratch a special off-road vehicle that has capabilities possessed by no other vehicle in the United States.
- Designed a special device that attaches to snow shovels, increasing efficiency by 16 percent.
- Consulted for a small businessman who was trying to perfect the design of a hydraulic pump. In a special letter of commendation, he said that he could not have finished the project without my help.
- Designed a special computer program that helps design latches. This program decreases design time by approximately 22 percent.

I will be graduating with a B.S. degree in mechanical engineering from Texas Tech University at the end of May.

I would like to visit your firm and meet you in a face-to-face interview to discuss further the details of my accomplishments and experience and how they might be utilized as an engineer with your firm.

Sincerely,

Howard A. Spalding
Telephone: (806) 555-1204

Ann E. Beach
904 Book Drive
Buffalo, New York 14214

May 9, 2001

Mrs. P.C. Finch
Director
Big Library
1750 Ninth 8treet
Buffalo, New York 14214

Dear Mrs. Finch:

While working as a librarian's assistant at State University of New York at Buffalo, I assisted 2,112 students and 368 faculty members in library research.

I am writing in case you need an assistant librarian. if you do, here are some other things I have done that may be of interest to you:

Cataloged more than 3,000 volumes at a major university library including classification, assignment dissection, and key word identification.

Completed 2 special seminars on the use of computers in information retrieval and designed a special computer program for this purpose for medium-sized libraries as a part of a university course.

Special-ordered 364 research volumes from 27 different publishers worldwide.

Managed the ordering, receipt, cataloging, and replacement of 217 professional magazines subscribed to by a university library.

I will receive my B.A. degree in library science from State University of New York at Buffalo in May.

I would like a personal interview to discuss further the details of my background and experience, as well as my qualifications for the position of assistant librarian.

Sincerely yours,

Ann E. Beach

Telephone: (212) 555-2897

Dana F. Brooks
757 Northern Avenue
Lincoln, Nebraska 68508

November 4, 2005

Mr. Peter W. O'Rourke
Director
Brookhaven Convalescent Home
5787 Woodrain Way
Lincoln, Nebraska 68508

Dear Mr. O'Rourke:

I developed 27 special dietary menus for individuals restricted to 9 separate diets.

I am writing in case you need a dietician for your facility. If so, you may be interested in some other things I have done:

- Completed research on the effectiveness of 9 nationally known diets given to 25,000 subjects in 31 different states.
- Worked as a part-time dietitian's assistant at Brookway Hospital, preparing dietary menus for 223 patients.
- Completed 5 longitudinal research studies on the varying effects of dietary factors on 7 subjects during a 6-month period.
- Advised and assisted 13 members of my sorority with their weight problems, which resulted in an average safe weight loss of 6.25 pounds per student.

I will be graduating with a B.A. degree in home economics, with a specialty in diet analysis, from the University of Nebraska in December of this year.

I would like to meet with you to further discuss the details of my background and qualifications for the position of dietitian.

Sincerely,

Dana F. Brooks

(402) 555-2001

Index